# SPIRITUAL ART THERAPY

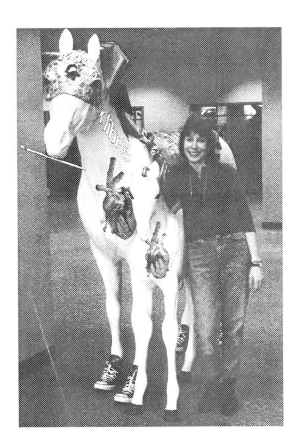

## ABOUT THE AUTHOR

**Ellen G. Horovitz, Ph.D., ATR-BC,** is Associate Professor and Director of Graduate Art Therapy at Nazareth College in Rochester, New York. She has had over twenty-five years of experience with myriad patient populations (inpatient, outpatient, day treatment, geriatric, visually handicapped, developmentally disabled, etc.) and specializes in family art therapy with the deaf. Dr. Horovitz currently is in private practice and works at the Speech Therapy and Aphasia Clinic at Nazareth College. She is the author of numerous articles and book chapters as well as *A Leap of Faith: The Call to Art.* Dr. Horovitz has served on the Education Program Approval Board (EPAB) of the American Art Therapy Association (AATA), Membership and Education Committees and Education Chair for AATA. She currently is on the Board of Directors for the American Art Therapy Association (AATA). Dr. Horovitz is also mother to Kaitlyn and Bryan Darby and is an avid painter and sculptor. She is featured above with her commissioned sculpture, "Horse Sense."

Second Edition

# SPIRITUAL ART THERAPY
## An Alternate Path

*By*

ELLEN G. HOROVITZ, PH.D., ATR-BC

*With a Foreword by*

**Werner I. Halpern, M.D.**
*Medical Director*
*Hillside Children's Center*
*Rochester, New York*

**Charles C Thomas**
PUBLISHER • LTD.
SPRINGFIELD • ILLINOIS • U.S.A.

*Published and Distributed Throughout the World by*

CHARLES C THOMAS • PUBLISHER, LTD.
2600 South First Street
Springfield, Illinois 62704

©2002 by CHARLES C THOMAS • PUBLISHER, LTD.

ISBN 0-398-07313-9 (hard)
ISBN 0-398-07314-7 (paper)

Library of Congress Catalog Card Number: 2002016172

*With* THOMAS BOOKS *careful attention is given to all details of manufacturing
and design. It is the Publisher's desire to present books that are satisfactory as to their
physical qualities and artistic possibilities and appropriate for their particular use.*
THOMAS BOOKS *will be true to those laws of quality that assure a good name
and good will.*

*Printed in the United States of America*
SR-R-3

**Library of Congress Cataloging-in-Publication Data**

Horovitz, Ellen G.
    Spiritual art therapy : an alternate path / by Ellen G. Horovitz ; with a foreword by Werner L. Halpern.
        p. cm.
Includes bibliographical references and index.
    ISBN 0-398-07313-9 (hard) -- ISBN 0-398-07314-7 (pbk.)
    1. Art therapy. 2. Psychotherapy--Religious aspects. 3. Mentally ill--Religious life. I. Title.
RC489.A7 H67 2002
616.89'1656--dc21
                                                                                                2002016172

*This is dedicated to the memory of my father, David M. Horovitz, and grandmother, Leah I. Billingkoff. Although they no longer take part of this life on earth, they always walk beside me in spirit. For that and the energy, which enabled me to create this work, I am eternally grateful.*

# FOREWORD

With the approach of the millennial year 2,000, apocalyptic beliefs about life on earth are likely to afflict many among both the devout and the unbelievers. To read meaning into existential events and landmarks, whether spawned by religious doctrine, piety, folklore, or superstition, remains at the very heart of the human struggle to fathom the seemingly impenetrable essence of man's relationship to creation and the Creator. The thinking person, healthy or not, questions the meaning and purpose of existence. In coping with this uncertainty, some take refuge in philosophy and some in ideologies, while others seek succor through religious or theologic belief systems. It must be apparent that none of these strivings bring genuine fulfillment unless people are also morally informed, since ritual piety and pious preachments often mask moral corruption.

Most clinicians sidestep their patients' or clients' existential concerns, usually out of conviction that these are not contributing significantly to adjustment problems and to mental disturbance, except in delusional individuals with mystical identifications. The spiritual realm, if acknowledged as part of a person's worldview, is often quickly assigned to officiants of whatever faith community is adhered to by the troubled individual. Indeed, pastoral counseling has become a discipline in its own right as it combines a blend of spiritual guidance and psychological insights.

In her treatise, *Spiritual Art Therapy: An Alternate Path,* Horovitz proposes that, on one level or another, each person is a seeker of spiritual transcendence, although most hide this need even from themselves. She perceives this search to be a critical element in attempts to cope with life's traumata, specifically loss and grief, when people face the emotional work of accepting the inevitable. Such groping for spirituality arises from idiosyncratic struggles with putting to rest the feeling of remoteness from any divine authority. On the other hand, those reared and steeped in the joyful tradition of worship from youth may consider their spirituality as an organic aspect of religious identity shared with family and co-religionists, which has a healing potential. Thus, in the words of Martin Buber, "God dwells in all things as a germ and a possibility of being; He is actualized by the fervor with which He is experienced."

In this book, therapists are urged to take into account the existence of spiritual aspects of personality, both in terms of making proper assessments and more focused treatment plans for the people under their care. Although addressing itself chiefly to art therapists, the thrust of this opus is an attempt to sensitize all clinical practitioners to the spiritual dimensions of therapy. By drawing on sources in the literature of religion, psychodynamics, systems theory, sociology, art, and ethics, Horovitz lays a foundation for her mission, namely to find a way of discovering, and if possible, measuring clients' spiritual sensibilities and search for personal meaning of their relationship to God. Out of her own struggles with this relationship, she has fashioned an instrument, which tries to integrate theologic and psychologic principles. Although the Belief Art Therapy Assessment (BATA) is meant to be only one of the diagnostic tools used by art therapists, its value to other clinicians may have applications in its present form or with future modifications. Several chapters in this book illustrate the usefulness of the BATA with quite different case presentations.

Through the use of the BATA, Horovitz seeks to understand the particulars of a person's spirituality rather than describe abstractions as holiness and grace. The prophet Micah summed up the values and deeds, which define the practice of the spiritually faithful, namely to do justly, to love mercy, and to walk humbly with God. May we all aspire to this lofty goal!

Werner I. Halpern, M.D.
*Medical Director in 1994*
*Hillside Children's Center*
*Rochester, New York*

---

*Author's Note:* Dr. Halpern passed away long before this new edition was birthed. I am grateful for the time we spent together as colleagues and fellow artists. He was much revered and will be long remembered in my community as well as the psychiatric community.

# PREFACE TO THE SECOND EDITION

Ideas gel in strange ways: twelve years ago, the premise behind this book originated from a dream. And over the years, I have learned to pay attention to those subconscious entities. They inform me, inspire me, and propel me to fulfillment.

Years ago, after converting from Judaism to Catholicism, the priest at my local parish, roped me into teaching the Sunday preschoolers. Having been raised in Judaic customs, it amused me that a Jew, now practicing Catholicism, would be imprinting young Christian minds. Unsure of the task ahead, I had been preparing my lessons for weeks. Being the A-type personality that I am, on the eve of my first day, I combed over my lesson plans and double-checked everything. Then, I went to bed. But the next morning, just before rising, I had this dream. In the dream, God called out to me and asked me to throw away my lesson plans. Instead, the message received in my dream was that I was to ask the children to "draw, paint or sculpt what God *meant*" to them. Mind you, the instructions were very clear. As I swung my legs out of bed that next morning, and bolted upright, I mused to myself, "What the Hell was that about?"

As I dressed and prepared for my first Sunday preschool class, I was mystified by the dream but decided to throw caution to the wind: I heeded the instructions communicated to me. I was unsure of the outcome, but I knew somehow that I was on a different path. And that trajectory has continued for sometime. Indeed, ten years after the first publication of this book, I still walk a road paved by inquiry. Always in the learning state, I am fittingly employed as a professor, and continually find myself ambling this course; I am no more certain of where this will lead me than when I first traversed this way. Although, one thing is for sure: my luxury in discussing such spiritual matters with patients, students, and colleagues has contributed to a secondary gain. I have become a more enlightened person because of this pathway.

Indisputably, years later, the intent of this book still is to animate the spiritual dimension that exists within all of us and embrace its resource for growth and change. It is my firm belief that tapping into a person's belief system and spiritual dimension can provide clinicians with information that can impact both assessment and treatment.

As a family art therapist, I feel it is essential to ascertain this information in order to better serve the needs of the identified patient and the family system. Mourning issues and losses (Horovitz-Darby, 1991; Harvey, 1984) are often prioritized in a family systems approach to treatment. Indeed, investigating a family's belief system seems paramount in ascertaining nodal events and family member reactions to change and trauma. Consequently, this caused me to look at people's intrinsic belief and/or disbelief in God and how that impacted them within their family systems. Moreover, it caused me to look at humankind's faith system, as well as how people sought strength and meaning in life.

As a result, I initiated a review of the literature surveyed from the perspective of spirituality, mental health, and art therapy (Chapter 2). This revealed not only myriad theories and perspectives, but more importantly that this quest had invaded the minds of others on the same journey toward spiritual healing (Coles, 1990; Dombeck & Karl, 1987; McNiff, 1987; Moon, 1990; Ellison, 1983; Gordon, 1990; Maton, 1989; Walls, 1991; and Gartner et al., 1991, to mention a few). This was strangely comforting since this pilgrimage often rendered my closest colleagues to question not only my raison d'être (and sometimes, sanity) but also my methodology and obsession with the relevance of this topic to assessment and treatment.

As I meandered along this footpath, both subjects and friends warned me that my journey would be fraught with "doubting Thomases." In fact, one subject warned me that I would continually be tested as I traveled. He reminded me that not only would people doubt what I was actually writing, but also they might question me in such a way that perhaps I would begin to doubt myself.

In Gerald May's book, *Simply Sane, The Spirituality of Mental Health,* he also warned of such misfirings. He declared:

> That intrusive voice of sanity is most disquieting, so one tends to move rather quickly, to shut it up. . . . One can say, "Oh, that's my sense of insecurity talking." One can label one's sanity as insanity. . . . Never stopping to realize that those self-doubts are the most honest, most sincere voice we can hear. (1987, p. 2–3)

And so after almost fifty some odd years of life, I am finally becoming comfortable with that voice and in the words of May, I am at last "going sane." Yet the struggle to quiet that inner, doubting voice often intercepts. In fact, years ago, when I first attempted to write up a synopsis of this work for presentation, I meekly remarked to a trusted friend, "Do you think I should mention God in this or allude to the concept?" His remark awakened me. He simply stated, "Never be afraid to sing God's praises." Growing up as an analytically minded art therapist, I had cowered and done anything but openly discuss the potential of mixing up God and/or the inclusion of spirituality with the healing process of therapy. Until now.

In Chapter 1, I discuss the evolution of this book and how I embarked upon the inclusion of the spiritual dimension in assessment and treatment. Chapter 2 reviews the literature that encircles art therapy, mental health, and spirituality, and explores its impact on both assessment and treatment. Chapter 3 examines the use of the Belief Art Therapy Assessment (BATA) as an instrument for assessing the spiritual dimension of a patient. Chapter 4 highlights the interviews and use of the BATA with the clergy. Chapter 5 explores the use of the BATA with a "normal" adult artist population. Chapter 6 looks at spiritual art therapy for the purposes of both assessment and treatment of emotionally disturbed children and youth in residential treatment. Chapter 7 offers a case vignette which illustrates the use of spiritual art therapy with a suicidal anorectic bulimic. Chapter 8 summarizes my position and theosophy. Two new chapters, 9 and 10, have been added since the first printing in 1994. Chapter 9 examines the use of phototherapy as a means to investigate mourning and loss issues. Examples are proffered from my work with students as well as clients with varying diagnoses from Asperger's syndrome to aphasia. Chapter 10 explores humankind's search for inner and outer meaning, the devastating effects of the September 11, 2001 attack on America, as well as my own exploration of mourning and loss as it affected my resolve through my artwork. And finally, I asked one of my current patients (from my private practice) to write the prologue for this edition. The reason for this is that she came to my practice *because* she had read my books and as a result wanted to work with me. Since she is a talented photographic artist in her own right, and studying to enter the field of clinical psychology, I thought that she could offer yet another perspective of this work that we do. For the art of being spiritual with oneself and one's patients involves empathic listening and co-creation.

The book, although finalized in Chapter 10, is by no means completed since inclusion of the spiritual dimension in assessment and treatment is a life-long struggle. I am committed to this work and feel that this treatise is merely an axis point. Feel free to embark and continue the dialogue.

Dr. Ellen G. Horovitz, ATR-BC
*Director of Graduate Art Therapy*
*c/o Nazareth College*
*4245 East Avenue*
*Rochester, New York 14618*

# PROLOGUE FROM A CLIENT

One summer evening, a few months ago, I became acutely aware of what was missing in my life–a teacher/master/mentor of sorts. They say "when the student is ready, the teacher will appear," and I felt ready. My graduate advisor and my therapist were not quite it. I wanted somebody to guide me through a journey of self-discovery and transformation. Looking at the starry sky through the slanted skylight in my living room, I prayed for this new person to come into my life. In the week that ensued, nothing happened, and I thought my prayer went unanswered. It took me a while to realize that in fact it was answered very shortly thereafter. It started with visiting the Nazareth Art Therapy website at the suggestion of a friend later that same week. I was just browsing when I read about Ellen's class on phototherapy, and found the topic very much to my liking since photography is one of my greatest passions. I found the work that Ellen seemed to be doing quite exciting. Shortly thereafter, I read her books, *A Leap of Faith: The Call to Art and Spiritual Art Therapy: An Alternate Path*. I was intrigued to see a combination of psychology, art, and spirituality as an approach to healing and became convinced that this was what I personally needed. I contacted Ellen and worked out to be seen in her practice. I felt very excited and fortunate. A couple of months later, thinking back to my prayer, I realized that it had hence been granted, and I now had the guide I needed in my life journey.

I have a fair amount of experience as a client. Prior to Ellen, I had seen four therapists. My anxiety and existential concerns survived intact through psychodynamic, cognitive behavioral and "eclectic" approaches. My main problem in expressing myself to my former therapists was that I could only articulate in the language they understood–psychology. However, my psyche communicated itself in a different medium, art. Since I was old enough to write, I have used writing as a way to express myself. Periodically, I used drawing, and in the past six years, I have explored photography as a medium to reflect on my life. I create images that my psyche dictates to me. My previous therapists showed interest in my art, and looked at my self-portraits with curiosity, and even admiration, However, the message behind the art remained impervious to them. They didn't get what art was for me, and what it did for my psyche, and above all, they didn't get the messages that came through it.

For my healing to occur, I need to be understood in my art, a part of me that was always shunned out and not understood in my family either. It is, therefore, difficult for me to make real progress fitting into the traditional therapeutic mold. The other aspect that I yearned for understanding was spirituality. What I needed again was more than cognitive validation, but true resonance. Spirituality is given full credit only by those who *are* spiritual. Yet, it seemed to me that a union of art, psychology, and spirituality would be unlikely, if not an impossible combination of skills and abilities to find in one therapist. What I needed to develop my personal process and work through my neurosis was somebody who could meet me and understand all three. One of my mentors, a spiritual artist, understood me quite well, but she is not a therapist. After four therapists, I had lost hope for a better understanding. My last therapist was also losing hope in me urging that an SSRI would rid me of my anxiety and my existential crisis. It was then that I came upon Ellen's work. When I read Ellen's books, I was in awe that somebody had put together the three ingredients that I yearned for in healing and development of my psyche.

I was very excited to start art therapy. I was delighted at the opportunity to create images that went with ideas. In my visual journals, creating an image meant creating a mirror that can reflect back, and the process of self-understanding could be furthered. Yet, these experiences had not prepared me for the intensity of art therapy. In my second session, Ellen asked me to create an image that depicted the way I felt inside. The image that arose in me was one of a woman bound to a tree. I painted the image loosely in watercolors (see Figure P-1).

Looking at it was scary and uncomfortable. There was the main issue right in front of me, and now in the eyes of another, as well. Though I can twist and turn my words, skirt issues, and avoid talking about what seems too painful to talk about, the starkness of that image revealed all. Ellen has reminded me of that image often, and has brought together how the same theme appears for me in other images or dreams that are at surface level quite different.

The psyche is drawn to what hurts, and what hurts is revealed in many ways in art therapy. Considering the quality of art is not of importance in this therapy, the images or clay products are pretty raw, primitive, and childlike. It is in these creations that I see painful memories take shape. Holding the clay product or looking at the images is not easy because they are tangible representations of issue or painful parts of me. Talking about them is an even bigger challenge. Yet, it is in the moments we talk about these things, that I

Figure P–1. "Bound."

feel my feelings and that internal shift starts to happen. The journey has begun.

Though I have seen Ellen now for some 18 sessions, we haven't talked directly about spirituality. My healing process is not going to happen overnight, because how I came to my struggles didn't happen overnight either. It is hard to change a way of being that I learned for the first 20 years of my life and that selectively reinforced the next 10, and probably still do. My process goes slowly, and I feel that we have just taken the first steps. However, considering my existential struggles and the question how can one be fundamentally safe in a sometimes erratic, unfair, and unsafe world, the question always comes back to God. How can God let such things happen? How can I make sense of the world then? If prayer is so helpful and God so generous, how come my grandparents died at a very advanced age without seeing their prayers answered? Didn't they matter? How can I trust that my hopes and prayers will be answered? Didn't they matter? How can I trust that my hopes and prayers will be answered? How can I trust that I am safe and what I hold most dear will be always mine? Ultimately, beyond the loss, the anger and the mourning, beyond it all, the ultimate question is a spiritual one.

Engaging in therapy with Ellen has given me the assurance that I need to trust the process, and to trust that she can be with me in spiritual territory when the time comes. Jung believed that all his patients over the age of 30 needed spirituality to complete their healing. Beyond art and therapy, I'll need the spiritual component to make sense of the world that has been harsh and sweet to me. It is in the order of the universe, God, and soul that I have found the greatest solace in the past, however fleeting. It is there that I believe the antidote for my anxiety exists, too. Accessing all of that in therapy is the real gift. I wish that *Spiritual Art Therapy* gives other therapists the courage to incorporate art and spirituality into their work.

# ACKNOWLEDGMENTS

There are many people that I would like to acknowledge regarding this labor and invariably, I will probably leave some of them out: First, and foremost, I am indebted to the people who shared their innermost thoughts about their relationship or nonrelationship with God and as well permitted me passageway via their art projections; I am also grateful to my patients who have taught me the necessity of behaving spiritually; I am also thankful to numerous people who supported me in a multitude of ways—my sister, Nancy A. Bachrach; my brother-in-law, Orin Wechsberg; my brother, Len H. Horovitz, M.D.; my sister-in-law, Valerie Saalbach; my mother, Maida M. Horovitz; Laurie and Bruce Konte and John and Dawn Neel, for spiritually taking care of my children while I pursued this work; "Spin" Michael Darby; Carol Darby; Werner Halpern, M.D., who read the first edition of this manuscript and sustained me while challenging my thinking; Darlene Esposito, MS, ATR for her continual friendship; my video art teachers, Keith McManus (and the Visual Studies Workshop) and John Neel, my mentor in videography; Lucy Andrus, MS, ATR, who taught me the necessity of "taking time to coast"; Victoria Laneri, ATR, who held down the fort at work; Irene Rosner David, Ph.D., ATR-BC and Michael Franklin, ATR-BC, who offered me a mirror for reflection; Katie Collie, ATR, a source of great spirit and inspiration; Sandra B. Mitzner, M.D., who continually spewed reflective comments via psychotherapeutic containment; Tom Ferland, who even in his last days on this earth, never stopped supporting my work; Emily Krenichyn, my wonderful graduate assistant; Bill "Birdheart" Bray for "e" communiqué; my wonderful colleagues: Ron Netsky, MFA; Dr. Kay Marshman, and Dr. Dennis A. Silva; my children, Kaitlyn Leah Darby and Bryan James Darby, for the time they gave up their "MaBa." Finally, I would like to thank the late Payne E. L. Thomas for having the aplomb to accept this book for publication and Michael Thomas for his support in recreating this second edition.

# CONTENTS

# FIGURES

# SPIRITUAL ART THERAPY

# Chapter 1

# EVOLUTION OF A SPIRITUAL APPROACH TO COUNSELING

The more one forgets himself
– by giving himself to a cause to serve or another person to love
– the more human he is and the more he actualizes himself.

–Victor E. Frankl

In the beginning, I experienced an extraordinary surge of energy associated with the purpose behind this book. Yet, often I felt unworthy of the task as well as inept in my pursuit. In fact, several times before I began this book, I played with ideas of coauthoring it with another–an associate, a psychologist, a priest, anyone who would have more knowledge than I have about spirituality, mental health, and/or God. I suppose I was so overwhelmed by this task, that I felt sharing it with someone would protect me from my projected criticism. I felt not only inferior for such a formidable task, but also (quite honestly) unprepared in the Judeo-Christian sense to tackle such work. After all, I was hardly cut from the teachings of divinity school. But having been raised Jewish only to convert to Catholicism in my later years certainly gave me an edge on guilt and the original sin. After all, I had enough guilt for both worlds. Yet, somehow, in my heart, I knew I had to tackle this alone and couldn't rest on others' coattails.

It is a difficult subject. Just the mere mention of God and psychotherapy is often enough to alienate one from several camps. But after all these years, I have decided that there really is only one camp from whose helm I derive comfort. Still, allowing God's work to infiltrate my existence as a therapist and clinician was simply uncharted territory, and, I might add a continuous struggle. This was due not only to my conflicts with associates but more alarmingly to my own resistance. In the words of Father Paul, an Indian priest, whom I tested: "The distinguishing of humanity that doesn't permit the mingling of God. . . . my own self interests . . . my own motives . . . those are times I keep God away. . . . The closer you are to God, the more you'll be tested, the more that humanity comes to your mind and that is quite testing. So the struggle is always there. That struggle is possible to keep God away from you. You can't really sustain that struggle and realize that God is in there waiting." And, how true that is. To continue the battle is exhausting and akin to anxiety, which exerts an inordinate amount of counterproductive, negative energy. Yet surrendering one's existence and succumbing to such ministry is enormously difficult in the face of the challenging opposition.

## EARLY STAGES

Formerly, I intended the Belief Art Therapy Assessment (described in Chapter 3) to be a phenomenological investigation of people's belief (or disbelief) in God and how that theosophy impacted them as they functioned both within their families and society. Nevertheless, it became clear that there were numerous factors that also needed to be configured. Yet, the ability to test subjects was not as clear cut as one might think. Because of the religiosity, it was not possible to gather information and test subjects in the usual manner.

For example, requests to administer this test were naturally rejected by the public school sector. So as a result, acquiring the information from a small batch of subjects from varied religious backgrounds was my only recourse. My hope was that the test be "ecumenical, eclectic, and empirical" as described by Bergin (1991). He proposed the following inclusion of spiritual orientations in the strategies for assessment and eventual treatment: (1) a conceptualization of the spiritual within the human experience; (2) a moral frame of reference, concluding that therapy is not value-free, suggesting universal limitations for human behavior; and (3) the use of spiritual techniques to improve the practice of psychotherapy.

In an attempt to incorporate these elements, I developed an interview format (which will be presented in Chapter 3) that preceded the actual BATA. Conducting these questions enabled me to ascertain background information, which not only summarized a subject's spirituality and religiosity but also gauged nodal events that may have contributed to the person's belief system and/or change in belief system. Yet it became crystal clear that a subject's responses to these questions could be both saccharine and/or superficial. So, it became necessary to conduct the BATA *only* when the patient questioned his belief system and after other diagnostic tests had been administered. The reason was twofold: (a) this is predicated on the patient's lead and (b) the previous tests offer the administrant enough sense of a patient's operational functioning to rule out false or misleading responses to the interview component of the BATA.

Not only age, sex, population, religion, et cetera are considered but more specifically, common icons that seemed to be appearing in the responses of the subjects. Some of the symbols were of no surprise both from an historical and psychological perspective. Yet what was truly amazing was how these symbols seemed to cut across the different strata of the populations surveyed. And so in addition to the literature review, there was the overwhelming task of collating the symbols and attempting to decipher their meaning, even if that meant "imagicide" (Moon, 1990). But it became all too clear that analyzing this data, while possibly quite relevant information, took a back seat to interviewing people and gathering information that could impact the inclusion of the person's spiritual component in treatment. It seemed that talking to people about God's impact in their lives was more relative to the quest then collating the symbols and analyzing the results. The data merely punctuated the study. But the discussions generated spirit. The essence of the art was to transliterate this language.

## INITIAL IMPRESSIONS

The first person that I tested was four years old; his name was John, and his religion was Roman Catholic. When I asked him to draw, paint, or sculpt what it was that God meant to him, he began to draw a symbol that had three distinctly closed elevations. It was colored in a bright yellow that seemed to exude light. When he finished, I politely asked him to explain his drawing. He stated quite matter-of-factly (and as if I should know) that it was a "crown." And I went on to ask him "how a crown meant God to (him)?" And just as certainly as he drew it, he replied, "A crown is a treasure and God is a treasure to me" (Figure 1-1). The simplicity and eloquence that he imparted through his meaning astounded me. I knew right then and there that this journey was going to be like no other. It was also abundantly clear that the spiritual dimension was linked to an ethical basis of human existence. Because of that truism, pursuing the spiritual dimension always needs to be tempered within the ethical confines of one's belief system.

The conversations with subjects of this study have left me abashed, amazed, and inspired. It has also confirmed my suspicions that when a patient has no one to turn to either through adversity or choice, often times the last

Figure 1-1. John's treasure.

stopping ground is God. I have witnessed this not only in my patient's lives, but also more importantly, in my own.

I remember all too painfully the accidental death of my father and surrounding aftermath. Because of extenuating circumstances, there was little to no time to truly mourn my losses, except when I went to temple. As I went to the *minyan* service for my father (a daily ritual which mourns the dead until the first anniversary of the death), I always weakened. I'm not sure if I could attribute this to being in the house of God, the Hebrew rituals, or just taking part in the *kaddish* (daily prayer for the dead), but something allowed me to breakdown, cry, and air my losses. Not even my therapist's office offered me such solace. To this day, whenever I enter church or temple, I am reduced to my senses.

Yet this is really not an anomaly—others, too, have experienced solace when in the house of God. But for some, the communion with God be it in a church or temple, has caused enormous duress. In my private practice, this often bridled recovery. Almost all of my patients were Catholic, all of them were struggling with mourning and loss (although the etiologies were quite varied) and all were grappling with their relationship or nonrelationship with God. Naturally, these similarities made me quite curious. My first step was to ask the priest of my parish what he thought about the preponderance of Catholics seeking my counsel as well as the primacy of their unrest regarding their relationship with God. His response, "We're all screwed up!" while stated in jest, was not far off the mark.

I pondered this for sometime (about six years) and while I continued to chip away at my practice and my patients' issues, I realized there had to be more to this than mere coincidence. This brought me back to a time of unrest within my own therapy and simultaneous controversy with God. I remembered sitting in my therapist's office and discussing my anger with God. My therapist questioned my debate over whether or not to seek counsel from my priest or from her. Naturally, she chalked up a portion of my battle to the age-old theory of patient/therapist resistance (a.k.a. negative transference). But, it was more than that. The aversion to my therapist and simultaneous disfavor for my priest was not just therapeutic resistance and discomfort with confession but more significantly, it was an abreaction to God and spiritual development. Unfortunately, either my therapist never figured this out or chose not to interpret this directly to me. But, I finally stumbled upon this truism years later when I encountered similar combat through my patients' warring with God and spirituality. In writing about spirituality, Jaoudi (1993) stated many truisms that hit home. Specifically, she stated:

> Psychology is the detergent, which will eventually lead us into the realm developing a solid spirituality. Psychology opens and cleanses us; spirituality leads us into freedom; . . . The deconditioning path, the path of letting go of everything, is the path to receiving that which is so much greater than the unreal possessions of the conditioned ego . . . The primary work is to come closer to God, and to share that love with humanity and all of creation. Secondary characteristics will indeed appear, but one is to either hide them, or only use them to further the work of mercy. (pp. 23–25)

Hence, I realized that if I had been privy to my patients' clashes with God and/or spiritual struggle from the inception of treatment, perhaps I would have handled their treatment differently. It became apparent that a tool should be developed that could assess one's belief system, gauge one's spirituality, and offer an avenue for treating the whole person—mind, body, and spirit. So, out of necessity, I developed the Belief Art Therapy Assessment. If it opens the door for even *one* person, then the work is not in vain. While the data could certainly be analyzed to ascertain commonality of symbols amongst certain populations, that was *not* the intent behind this work. Instead, the investigation was to provide an avenue for inquiry into one's belief and faith systems. The premise was to be inclusive of community since culture weaves a biologic thread that wefts our existence and indeed guides our actions. And so for the *doubting Thomases,* I offer spiritual art therapy not as a panacea but as a route for exploration, ministry, and perhaps health.

# Chapter 2

# ART THERAPY, MENTAL HEALTH AND SPIRITUALITY: WHERE THE TWAINS MEET

They prevented me in the day of my calamity:
but the LORD was my stay. He brought me forth also into a larger place;
he delivered me, because he delighted in me.

–Psalm 18: 18, 19

## SOME DEFINITIONS

Religiosity and belief have been juxtaposed by science and rational thinking. While they are closely related and certainly interface, they are distinctly different. Moreover, since the seventeenth century, Galileo affair, science and religion forged an unwritten contract of nonrelationship. Religious thinkers agreed that the "natural world" was the sole province of the scientists. And scientists agreed to keep their nose out of the "supernatural"– or for that matter anything to do with the spiritual. Verily, science circumscribed itself as "value-free."

According to Peck, ". . . there has been a profound separation between religion and science. This divorce . . . more often remarkably amicable–has decreed that the problem of evil should remain in the custody of religious thinkers. With few exceptions, scientists have not even sought visitation rights, if for no other reason than the fact that science is supposed to be value-free." Peck further espoused that for a variety of multifaceted reasons, this separation no longer works. He stated, "There are many compelling reasons for their reintegration–one of them being the problem of evil itself–even to the point of the creation of a science that is no longer value-free" (1983, p.40).

9

Today, this partnership has caused scientists and religious thinkers alike to reside as uneasy bedfellows. Yet, it was not always this way. The history of most culture declares an integration of science with religious and ritualized "spiritual" activities (Dombeck & Karl, 1987; Frank & Frank, 1991; Jung, 1965, Dearing, T., 1983). Alas, in the last century, there has been a profound departure from this plaited marriage. In fact, this duality has caused ministerial and health care professions to become formally distinct. The result has ranged from open hostility to mutual cooperation.

Indeed, the religious and spiritual needs have been entrusted to the clergy. Baptism, last rites, confirmation, communion, and even prayer have been relegated to religious leaders. This domain has created a fissure for any clinician who has faced a client's spiritual questions, struggle with faith, and/or desire for forgiveness. There have been several options:

1. ignoring the spiritual dimension of the patient;
2. chalking up the patient's thinking as floridly psychotic;
3. referring the patient to a clergy person without participating in that aspect of care (thus, defeating a systemic approach);
4. collaborating with a clergy person and working out an interdisciplinary approach to treatment;
5. or attempting to spiritually counsel the patient.

Dombeck and Karl, came up with these additional postulates:

1. Who should assess religious and spiritual needs, and how are these needs assessed by each profession?
2. Would an interdisciplinary approach increase the possibility for spiritual assessment and response to spiritual needs?
3. Is the assessment of spiritual needs important in making correct diagnoses? (1987, p. 184)

Truly, a holistic approach to a person's wellness includes mind, body, and spirit. And, the premise behind this book is to investigate these aforementioned options and questions. Thus, I am making the assumption that spiritual care is a legitimate part of health care. Even though the clergy has a specified role in this arena, I purport that the spiritual needs of a patient require attention and treatment by the entire health care team.

First, however, some definitions are necessary:

*Interdisciplinary* is defined as a process of combining the myriad talents and skills of professionals necessary to eradicate the problems of a person's condition and contribute to his overall recovery and health.

While related, the terms *religion* and *spiritual* are **not** synonymous:

*Religion*, an organized system of faith, is defined as an "organized body of thought and experience concerning the fundamental problems of existence."

*Spirituality* "deals with the life principle that pervades and animates a person's entire being, including emotional and volitional aspects of life. . . . The search for meaning and purpose through suffering and the need for forgiveness are elements of the spiritual life" (Dombeck & Karl, 1987, p. 184).

As well, the terms *faith* and *community* require both consideration and definition:

*Faith,* while often associated with the term belief, reflects confidence in the trust and value of a person, idea, or thing. Tradition imposed on a belief system gives *rise* to faith. According to the dictionary, faith has also been linked to a belief and trust in God as well as a religious conviction hinged to a system of religious principles and beliefs. However, one definition that is differentiated from religious dogma unites faith with a belief that does *not* rest on logical proof or material evidence.

*Community* demands inclusion since man interfaces with his cultural network and relies on this system for feedback, reinforcement, support, and oftentimes, for parameters within his individualized frame of reference. Ashbrook in his treatise, *be/come Community,* talked about our highway system as being the only true source of communal architecture since it "organizes, channels, connects and directs our separate yet independent living." In linking community with both a means and way in which to connect with others, he proposed that the means "enables us to break-out of the boxes in which we are trapped" (providing an instrument for our intentions) as well as a way to wed us to reality and other people (1971, pp. 72–73).

From a systemic perspective, an interdisciplinary and communal approach to treating an identified patient within a family systems framework is not only essential but also fundamental in the treatment of the whole person. Moreover, in order to accomplish such a formidable task, incorporating the spiritual and religious components into treatment requires a tool for assessing whatever nodal events contributed to the disorder and dis-ease of the person. While the Belief Art Therapy Assessment (described fully in Chapter 3) offers an instrument for estimation, the reader may not be comfortable with continued exploration of a patient's spiritual belief system. If, in fact, this is the case, *then* one needs to embrace an interdisciplinary approach and rely on the skills and talents of other professionals within the community.

## STARTING POINTS

Integrating art therapy with family therapy from a historical perspective requires a systemic orientation. On intake, the administrant needs to join with his patient(s) and construct a three generation genogram (Guerin & Pendagst,

1976). This historical perspective views the identified patient (IP) in context of the family's life cycle and allows the practitioner to review historical events that created the current symptomatology within the family's present condition. This enables the therapist to consider the relevancy of the underlying issues as outlined by the critical past events and issues. Moreover, it empowers the clinician with the armament necessary for adequately combating the issues with empathy and direction. With these tools, the clinician moves on to the next stage of assessing and diagnosing the IP in order to construct a hypothesis for treatment.

Now there are some art therapists who arguably contend that assessment and diagnosis is unnecessary for treatment. While assessment and diagnosis may not be the axis point for all art therapists, it is my contention that one cannot do adequate treatment without it. Would a doctor prescribe pharmaceutical medication without assessing and determining the causality? I think not. Assessment and diagnosis encompass the full range of the patient from a holistic perspective. Like the good doctor, exploring every avenue when pursuing the etiology of the system, is the hallmark of an able, well-armed clinician. And when wrestling with physical, psychological and/or emotional disorders and dis-ease, one needs all the accouterments he can muster. (Indeed "Dis" is an old Roman name for the mythological underworld. When considering how disease enters the body and finds an opening into health where functioning breakdowns, the concept of dis-comfort and dis-function seems quite applicable.)

A number of assessment tests abound, but for comparative purposes, I like to administer the following tests: (1) The House Tree Person (H-T-P) test (Buck, 1950, 1966); (2) The Kinetic Family Drawing test (K-F-D) (Burns & Kaufmann, 1972); (3) The Silver Drawing Test of Cognitive and Creative Skills (S-D-T) (Silver, 1992); (4) The Cognitive Art Therapy Assessment test (CATA) (Horovitz-Darby, 1988); and *when indicated*, the Belief Art Therapy Assessment test (BATA). (I underscore that I employ the BATA *only* when warranted. The reason is that when florid, psychotic thinking is present, conducting the test in its entirety can in fact exacerbate this condition, plaguing emotionally disturbed individuals. And, so I conduct the BATA *only* when the patient questions or brings up his belief/spiritual dimension on interview or within the aforementioned testing component. Moreover, it is conducted *only* when the information might lead to an improved understanding of the patient as opposed to contributing to further deterioration of his condition.) Furthermore, even after the patient reveals his spiritual struggle by way of the BATA, it is wholly possible that he may not be ready to explore his "spiritual dimension" since this involves abstract thinking. If, in fact, the patient's thinking is formal, rigid, and concrete, then the therapist needs to walk this line with trepidation and *always* respect the client's lead.

Conducting these tests offers me a vantage point for assessing treatment perspectives but I have discovered that no matter what the etiology or current condition of the IP, it is always imperative to return to the origins of mourning and loss (Horovitz-Darby, 1991). For the benchmark in exploring mourning and loss sets the table for spiritual recovery and mental health.

In abiding by this, one is reminded of the task beset by the universal Job. The biblical yarn of Job, who in one day lost all of his fortune, husbandry, and ten children, is a remarkable tale of a man who never lost faith in God. Even though he was tested by misfortune and destitution, Job's steadfast belief resulted in God reinstating his lot with additional riches, family, and good fortune. The moral, that through faith all can be restored, is strong medicine.

## LANGUAGE SYSTEMS, MOURNING, AND LOSS

Analyzing a family system via its communication style is crucial to family therapy with any population. For example, modes of communication employed by family members may vary and the range of language systems may be expansive, circumscribed, bimodal, or virtually absent (Horovitz-Darby, 1991). This finding cannot be underestimated. Separate communication modes contribute to alienation, isolation, and linear punctuation. Thus, operating within an individual versus a communal construct can exacerbate, heighten, and contribute to such a divisive position. Instead, transcending toward a faith community, be it secular or universal, might help restore holistic functioning.

In order to create such "circular reciprocity" (Arrington, 1991) and envelop heteromorphic thinking, one needs to shake up the system—reframe it, if you will. Yet, any attempt to recast the family communication system threatens the homeostasis and established "balance of power" among family members (Harvey, 1984).

Investigating the distribution of labor and power, which sustains the family myth of the identified patient as the root cause aides the clinician in recasting the IP as no longer "sick." Moreover, while analyzing this situation, the therapist generally runs amuck mourning and loss issues that somehow are never resolved. Although the origin of these issues always varies, deep in the chronological, time line of the family, it can always be found. And, so before a patient or system can be edged toward recovery, inspection and perusal are required to repair the damage. Like the mechanic attempting to decipher the misfirings of an engine, the therapist must begin to unseat these fittings and reassemble the engine parts with doses of empathy and emotional resonance.

Beginning with these losses reconnects the patient to his very origin of disease (e.g., symptomatic discomfort) and sets the stage for inclusion of the spiritual dimension. If one skips over these elements too quickly, then the work is not only hampered but spiritual evolution is impeded. As Moore suggests, the work of therapists would change radically "if we thought about it as ongoing care rather than as a quest for a cure" (1992, p.19).

Whether or not the therapist chooses to employ this work from the perspective of invoking God or God's imagery is a matter determined by the patient and the clinician; but clearly, the therapist needs to move through this strata mindful of the patient's apprehensions and defenses. Indeed, it becomes an approach-avoidance dance where often the patient (and supportive therapist) take two steps forward and two steps backward. While mourning is restoration in and of itself, leveling the pain attached to loss is tantamount to all the issues and symptoms, which so cleverly arise from this tenacious grasp. But I contend that focusing on loss and mourning issues cannot be ignored and **has** to be the principal step in recovery. Without this primacy, there may be change, but *not* resolution or evolution. Instead, the symptoms will manifest again and again until the feelings connected to these losses are aired, examined, and most importantly *accepted*. It is then and **only** then that the real work can begin.

## THE SEARCH FOR MEANING

Psychoanalysts and psychiatrists who concur with the stance adopted by Freud in his *History of an Illusion,* described religious and spiritual beliefs as neurotic and pathological (Ahlskog, 1990). The "imago," as delineated by Freud, incorporated various aspects of a child's parental perceptions, including religious orientation and beliefs. Alas, he viewed such dogma as overcompensation for feelings of universal powerlessness and the infantile desire for an eternally nurturing presence, e.g., God. Health was viewed as abandonment of such principles. Moreover, much of the subsequent psychoanalytic literature centered on distorted representations and employment of religious beliefs, such as religious delusions in psychotic individuals (Meissner, 1992). As well, art therapists proclaimed religious symbols arising in the artwork of severely disturbed individuals (Cerricola, 1975). Both Cerricola (1975) and Meissner (1992) defined the formal qualities of a religious belief system as contributing to pathological closedness, rigidity, and narrowness.

In contrast to this reasoning is the induction that low levels of religiosity have often been associated with disorders of over control (Gartner et al., 1991). (While religion may be involved in pathology (and art creation), it may not be implicated for those individuals who see themselves as religiously or spiritually oriented.) Likewise, Bergin (1991) reviewed the empirical literature and ascertained that there was no reason to equate religiosity with mental illness. Indeed, he was able to track a genuine relationship between other variables associated with mental health (e.g., lack of anxiety) and a basic religious orientation.

Accordingly, Frankl's (1984) tenet and search for meaning in one's life is the primary motivational force in humankind. Yet one needs to evaluate what Frankl means by primary motivational force since this can eventuate both positive and negative ramifications. History need only reminds us of the power wielded by Adolph Hitler and the cults of people like David Koresh. Thus, one's *ethics* always must be considered and underscored in order to rule out the type of mysticism that perpetuates itself in the doings of pure, unadulterated evil.

In contrast to Freud's pleasure principle and imago assumption, Frankl equates this journey as a *will to meaning*. His adherence to the principle of Logotherapy differs from Psychoanalysis insofar it considers man a being whose fundamental interest consists in executing a *meaning* as opposed to mere gratification and satisfaction derived from drives, instincts, the pleasure seeking principle or the concept of eros and thanatos. His concept of mental health therefore seems to be a constant state of flux based on a certain degree of tension between what one has already achieved and what one still ought to accomplish, "the gap between what one is and what one should become" (p. 110). Indeed, he contends that the ". . . true meaning of life is to be discovered in the world rather than within man or his own psyche. . . . In other words, self actualization is only possible as a side-effect of self transcendence" (p. 115). Again, however, one is reminded of Koresh and Hitler, and thus this idea of self-transcendence and psychological mysticism needs to be tempered with a dose of ethics.

McDargh (1983) implies two reasons for humans seeking the transcendent: (1) the threat of dissolution forces people to recognize their finite and limited stay on earth while (2) the human character continually questions the transcendent, "incomprehensible mystery of God" (p. 112). McDargh goes on to discuss this "openness to mystery" as a tool for empowering the client to reshape his experiences. Yet as Moon (1992) aptly points out: "It is only through experience that God images will be affected, refined, (and) reshaped."

She offers engagement with the art materials as the conduit for embracing radical openness to mystery and engagement with the transcendent. Similarly, she forewarns others of the great importance of this tryst with patients around their God representations, both via verbal and pictorial expression.

Additionally, Asch (1985) proclaims animistic, magical thinking to be a component of all human reasoning which invites a mystical view of psychological phenomena. Although Asch proclaims that this is a developmental stage, which most outgrow, the question remains why we need to outgrow something, which is in fact so primal. Capell's unpublished master's thesis also concurs with these findings. She proclaims:

> Special consideration must be given when working with clients whose belief systems and concepts of illness are either delusional or at odds with those of the therapist. When a client perceives to be involved in a personal struggle with the devil due to . . . religious or cultural frame of reference, or believes to be controlled by evil forces . . . transcultural considerations must be incorporated into treatment. (1991, p. 31)

Henricson-Cullberg's work with a borderline patient who asserted that she was "possessed" by the devil equates demonic possession with negative internalized objects. Through the ministry of religious terms (although Henricson-Cullberg was by statement, not a religious person), she encouraged the client to replace her fear of the devil by belief in a supportive, forgiving God. Not unlike Freud, she utilized God as a projection of the patients inner struggles and introjects. She determined:

> . . . a structural change may have taken place as a result of the integration of the aggressive component. . . . At one level, God may be the idealized object with a holding function, at another the picture of God diversified and developed in a more mature way. The picture of God we make for ourselves is probably parallel to the development of our inner objects. (1984, p. 193)

In reviewing the theoretical literature on development as applied to religious and moral aspects of personality development, Worthington (1989) proposed various spiritual implications for normative and non-normative life transitions, which included consideration of the individual's specific development and their position within their life cycle. While he equated the failure to assess an individual's religious development as equivalent to the failure to assess meaning to a person's gender, race, or sexual orientation, he did not differentiate between a person's ability to be moral without being spiritual, a rather important point. Yet, Worthington did note the degree of assessment as dependent on two variables: (a) the degree of supposed religious involvement and (b) the practitioner's general assessment philosophy. Worthington described the problem of addressing spiritual and religious concerns only as they arose in treatment. One problem with this wait-and-see approach is that this requires that the client bring these concerns to the forefront. Furthermore, he contends that deeply religious persons may be disinclined to introduce such material for fear of lack of understanding, requiring them to act in a manner which contradicts inherent beliefs in addition to devaluing spiritual phenomena as a way of operating. So the only clear-cut answer to this dilemma is to operate on a case by case basis and always respect the client's lead, introducing the topic *only* when it will truly serve the needs of the patient. Naturally, the therapist can only determine this session by session.

## SPIRITUAL AND MENTAL HEALTH CONNECTIONS

According to Hettler (1979, 1991), wellness can be compartmentalized into six major dimensions: intellectual, emotional, physical, social, occupational, and spiritual. (While the spiritual dimension is clearly an important addition, it is odd that Hettler failed to include both a developmental and communal component.) Spiritual wellness has recently surfaced in the literature of health care and counseling and exacted considerable interest. Nevertheless, when compared to the other five dimensions, it has largely been ignored due to not only lack of clarity but also debate about its definition, application, and province. Indeed, it was noted by Allen and Yarian (1981) that the (counseling) profession in fact should not only define spiritual wellness but also incorporate and integrate its construct within the field of health care. While the pastoral counseling profession has long been attending to the spiritual dimension, Allen and Yarian concur with Hettler's stance that it be consolidated within the other counseling disciplines.

Theoretically there are at least two major pathways through which spiritual support can impact treatment: (1) the "cognitive meditation" pathway posits that spiritual support contributes to the adoption of a positive cognitive appraisal of the meaning and implication of negative life events via positive reframing and elongates the stress response, leading to enhanced emotional adjustment and (2) the "emotional support" pathway posits that perceptions of being loved, cared, and valued by God directly leads to enhanced self-esteem as well as reduction of negative affect for individuals vulnerable to high levels of stress (Wright et al., 1985; Newman & Pargament, 1987; Spilka & Schmidt, 1983). While Cohen and Wills (1985) implicate alternative pathways for social support, Maton (1989) asserts that spiritual support exerts an influence on well-being independent of perceived social support. Maton continues by defining "spiritual support" as affirming perceptions not limited solely to relationships with other people but to varying extents relationships with God.

Still other avenues, such as rabbinical teachings, suggest human relationships to God (resulting in these affirming perceptions) are enacted through good deeds accomplished (preferably) incognito. One wonders how such spiritual support would be acquired within this construct? In this case, a per-

son would not benefit from communal reinforcement of his works and perhaps would not exact the type of spiritual support suggested by Maton. Alas,
the question remains if basking in God's knowledge would be enough to contribute to this spiritual support matrix? While the Christian doctrines would
affirmably proclaim a joyous "Yes!" to such a position, those who truly need
the communal support of their faith community might experience this as a
more difficult path to follow.

Nevertheless, the aforementioned research suggests that spiritual support
may contribute to well-being through enhancing self-esteem and reducing
negative affect (via the "emotional support" pathway) or through repairing
positive and adaptive appraisals of the meaning of a traumatic affliction (via
the "cognitive meditation" pathway). According to Maton:

> From an applied perspective, these results also suggest a need for research
> focused on the influence of therapists in general, and of religious or pastoral cli-
> nicians in particular, on perceptions of spiritual support in clients undergoing
> stressful life events. (1989, p. 321)

In discussing what we believe in, Tart proposed two more pathways to
overcome our "world simulator" and get in better touch with reality: the first
involves attention-training processes that promote a volitional and more
direct access to input (e.g., insight meditation—observing the rapid flow of
experience in its totality without becoming lost in limited aspects of it); the
second or complementary method involves focused insights into the particular contents of "your world-simulation process and (forcing) to consciousness
the *specifics* of how you construct your experienced world" (1989, p. 216).

However, care must be taken with patients whose egos are so fractured
and/or reduced, that in using these "emotional support," "cognitive meditation," "attention-training processes," and/or "world-simulation processes"
that one doesn't subvert treatment to a higher power and induce psychosis or
cult-like behavior.

## RELIGIOUS APPLICATIONS

According to Simon (1989), authentic spirituality contains a price: understanding, work, and suffering. While his five-fold program (prayer, spiritual
reading, practice of virtue (specifically love and good works), reception of
sacraments (daily if possible), and self-denial) clearly arises out of Catholic
doctrines, his end result purports to lead towards transformation of the personality and increased productivity.

Recommending communication within a Biblical milieu, Young (1984)
states that one need only be familiar with the concept of forgiveness as found

in the Bible when applying his particular process of RET (Rationale Emotive Therapy) with extremely religious clients. While he doesn't dispute literal doctrines, he instead applies cognitive strategies to redefine the version of the Scriptures in a rational and beneficial manner.

Ellison (1991) confirms the influence of religious variables on subjective well-being. Several of his findings are especially noteworthy. First, firm religious beliefs seem to significantly enhance both the cognitive and affective perceptions of life quality despite the steadfast control over the influence of public and private religious engagement. Second, while previous research focused on church attendance and private reverence, religiosity patterns contributed to the well-being by indirectly reinforcing religious beliefs and world views. Third, religious faith buffers the negative effects on the trauma of well-being. Fourth, the study sustains the view that religious symbols and beliefs provide an interpretative arena through which individuals can make sense of everyday life. Religious symbols and values may mold: "(1) the appraisal of those potentially stressful life events which occur as less threatening and (2) the assessment of individual capacities to cope successfully" (1991, p. 90).

While Ellison's study attests to religious faith as a buffer to trauma, faith and spirituality are not the same things. As I have stated within the definition of faith, tradition imposed on a belief system gives rise to faith. The spiritual realm incorporates but also transcends faith as an altered ego state, which may have adaptive or maladaptive implications. It is in this that practitioners need to tread carefully and ethically.

Moore (1992) takes the potential of religion a step further than most and propounds that a ". . . person who turns to the Bible as a compendium of insight into the nature of soul does not need psychology." But he continues to warn against using the Bible for moral certainty, miraculous proofs of faith, or for avoidance of doubt and anxiety in making difficult life choices. He contends that ". . . all spheres of life have deep roots in the mysteries of the soul, and therefore are holy" (pp. 238–242). Finally, he suggests that we learn from other cultures, specifically art, religion, and philosophy, and ". . . replace modernist psychology with care of the soul" in order to build a culture sensitive to the matters of the heart" (p. 284). Although idealistically this might work in a land of utopia, to throw out the baby (psychology) with the bath water seems inherently dangerous. Like others who propose such drastic measures, this concept needs to be taken with a grain of ethical salt.

Gordon's treatise, *Holistic Medicine and Mental Health Practice* (1990), predicts a number of changes affecting both the roles of the patient and clinician in treatment. He concludes that mental health's role will be redefined: no longer will the therapist function as the tabula rasa. This "resacralisation" of the therapeutic role (via spiritual education) will allow practitioners to regard themselves as servants of a larger spiritual reality–conceived of as God or nature—of which they and their patients are a part. The result will recast clinicians as vehicles for healing rather than as agents for change.

Moreover, they will view themselves as co-participants in this life-affirming process and restore their patient's harmony as well as their own. Indeed, this "role change" will induce a changed attitude toward mental health practice and toward psychiatric disorders: This spiritual perspective which embraces life as a series of occasions for self-growth and knowledge offers an avenue for accomplishing changes ordered by dis-ease. This approach clearly can be utilized in working with people with adjustment disorders, since this doctrine employs the strengthening of the ego and application of self-help techniques. Verily, this progression might also work well with biological disorders (for example depression, panic disorders, and cyclothymic disorders) treated with psychopharmacological formulas. It is a reminder that certain characteristics whether psychological and/or biological are subject to the same attitudinal influences as adjustment disorders—or as cardiovascular disease or cancer.

Gordon also contends that along with other approaches, meditation, a primary tool for the development of spirituality, may well be taught and prescribed as medicine now is. He specifically asserts that more "individualized forms of comprehensive treatment" will be developed encompassing an increase in both the numbers and kinds of modalities tailored to the needs of the individual client.

Changes in role, approach, services, and research will depend on new modes of training, which would by definition need to include an opportunity to study the work of healers in other cultures. This would ensure that mental health practice will be predicated on the transformation of practitioners. Gordon proposes that:

> The aim of this transformation will be the attainment of something like the authenticity or enlightenment that has so often been described in the world's scriptures—including the Bible, Buddhist sutras, and the Taoist parables. According to these accounts, the person who is genuinely the servant of the divine, as well as the human, is characterized by a combination of detachment and compassion, discernment and flexibility, humility and playfulness. The healer has an indefinable yet distinctly reassuring presence that, no matter what the problem, all is well. Interestingly, such a state seems in many ways a realized version both of the ideals of the patient's projections onto their therapists and of the ideal therapist. (1990, p. 368)

In this lies the fundamental danger of casting humans into the position of seeking nirvana. Alas, this has little to do with God or nature as both incorporate demands on the living to struggle towards perfection rather than achieve it. To achieve perfection is to be God. Instead, the task of human beings is to *simulate* God-like traits as perceived in personal theosophy. Otherwise, the course goes astray and contributes to madness.

## THE NATURE OF SPIRITUALITY

Several psychological archetypes included spirituality in their concepts of the nature of persons. In Maslow's theory of self-actualization (1971), he incorporates the spiritual life as a defining characteristic of human nature. His study of optimally functioning people is labeled as "transcendent self-actualizers." Transcenders (if positive) as opposed to mere self-actualizers demonstrate different characteristics which place them in a distinct realm of functioning. For example, their characteristics include a holistic perspective about the world, a natural drive towards synergy and cooperative efforts (be it intrapsychic, interpersonal, and intracultural), behavior motivated by intrinsic truth, goodness, and unity, a greater veneration for pinnacle experiences, an attitude of equality toward others, the ability to be aware of self-identity and transcend beyond the ego self, the language of "Being," and finally, the inclusion of sacredness toward every person and every living thing. Coincidentally, some of these same characteristics can be found in both the Old and New Testaments when referring to God.

Psychosynthesis, postulated by Assagioli (1965), hypothesizes the construct of a "higher consciousness" or "superconsciousness" which exists in all humans. He suggests that this area of the psyche receives ". . . our higher intuitions and aspirations—artistic . . . scientific, ethical imperatives and urges to humanitarian (action) . . . the source of higher feelings . . . of genius and of the states of contemplation, illumination and ecstasy" (p. 17). In a later work, he further espouses:

> "Spiritual" refers not only to experiences traditionally considered religious but to *all* the states of awareness, all the human functions and activities which have as their common denominator the possession of *values* higher than average. (1989, p. 30)

(Yet, exactly what Assagioli means by average values is never clearly defined. And so these values need to be individually determined by the reader.)

In Jung's well-known work *Memories, Dreams and Reflections* (1965), he continually grapples with the duality and struggle for spiritual attainment. He determines that one, perforce, has to be totally abandoned to God in order to fulfill his will (p. 40). The struggle to accept this position created a fissure in his personality, which he affectionately referred to as personalities No. 1 and No. 2. He proposes that this split, while not *dissociation* in the medical sense, is played out in every individual. According to Jung, personality No. 2, the "other" personality of higher consciousness and inner peace, is perceived only by the very few. Moreover, he asserts: "Most people's conscious under-

standing is not sufficient to realize that (this) is also what they are" (p. 45).
Jung felt "enjoined" with God and doing God's work. In his words:

> . . . I was no longer alone, I was outside time; I belonged to the centuries; and
> He who then gave answer was He who had always been , who had been before
> my birth. He who was always there. These talks with the "Other" were my pro-
> foundest experiences: on the one hand a bloody struggle, on the other hand
> supreme ecstasy. (1965, p. 48)

It is with this struggle that I can so readily identify. Espousing similar feelings to many colleagues has often been met with fraught concern. And then
there have been those who have understood this journey; to quote one colleague, Carol Bowen, "It's like coming home." And, as Jung maintains:

> My entire youth can be understood in terms of this secret. It induced in me an
> almost unendurable loneliness. My one great achievement during those years
> was that I resisted the temptation to talk to anyone. Thus the pattern of my rela-
> tionship to the world was already prefigured: today as then I am a solitary,
> because I know things and must hint at things which other people do not know,
> and usually do not even want to know. (1965, pp. 41–42)

Hammer (1990) discusses the necessity of "loosening one's grip on rationality" in order to help clients validate their feelings and focus on affect. (But
if taken literally, "loosening one's grip on rationality" would be detrimental
and lead perforce to psychosis. Here, I propose that the reader insert "linear
rationality" into the equation in order to deflect such meaning.) In speaking
about the analyst's experience as a flash of insight, he comments:

> It is felt as a passive opening of oneself to receive that which comes. As we lis-
> ten to the patient's material with "hovering attention," not only do we feel a
> conscious urge to reach out for its meaning and its emotional subtleties, but
> when our sensibilities are tuning in, we experience it as something in the mate-
> rial reaching out to us. (p. 97)

Perhaps what Hammer is suggesting here is the nature of our synthetic
function. Tuning into these sensibilities creates a pathway of heightened
awareness for dynamic interplay with the client.

Ekstein (1959) also concurs with this position and extends this thinking by
insinuating that one needs to trust his preconscious and surrender ordinary,
secondary process thinking in order to permit thought processes which stem
from archaic levels to predicate authentic, psychoanalytic work. Capitalizing
on this maxim, Hammer (1990) aptly states that we function more creatively
not when we focus our concentration but when we "relax it—when we actually *unfocus concentration*" (p. 98). Hammer, in fact, tunes into the marginal ideas,
peripheral feelings, and physical sensations of the patient as well as his own.
He describes this posture as being open and resonating with the patient and

allowing for pictures to form in his "creative zones; an image crystallizes, reflecting the patient's experience" (p. 99).

Being open to this kind of experience, borders on countertransference since in fact the therapist enlists his own projections of the patient's state in unraveling and releasing authentic affect. Yet this is the premise of spiritual underpinnings. But as Assagioli (1989) asserts: in the realm of spiritual development, one cannot help another past one's own level of development. And, so in order to undertake such work, one must start from within.

Nevertheless, allowing oneself passageway into such a journey of dependence on intuition, projection, and resonance of the patient's position is dangerous territory. First and foremost, this approach although elucidating can be confusing and dangerous for an incipient art therapist because the approach is both amorphous and idiosyncratic. But no matter how much training and supervision occurs, when all is said and done, seasoned clinicians often end up operating from within their own construct due to prejudicial belief systems. So why not teach therapists to trust this intuitive life force that pervades and animates our very being? If, instead of ignoring this principle, we encourage its blossom, it can be tempered, wrestled, and confronted in the context of constructive supervision. The result might just lead to emotional resonance for both therapist and patient. But how can this be accomplished? One of the major aspects of a "false personality," as outlined by Tart, is that one does not *truly* choose concepts, feelings, and roles for identification. Instead, the "enculturation process–the induction of consensus trance . . . cajole(s) and condition(s)" our identification with many roles, ideas, people, causes, and values that may actually oppose a true, essential self (1989, p. 126). Since most supervisory situations don't often nurture the clinician's need for such soul-searching direction, perhaps the most sincere course would be continued dialogue within the communal structure of a supervision group predicated entirely for this purpose. Perhaps this *community* could then embrace such undisciplined thinking and court positive transformation within the members. Just a thought.

## RELIGIOMAGICAL HEALING AND SHAMANISM

McNiff purported that today's art therapist engage in an ancient form of healing by offering patients a place for reintegration of the artistic senses, which in former times was an accepted way of life. He suggested that:

> . . . the ultimate transvaluation of experience involves the transformation of human suffering into a dramatization of the endurance and compassion of the human spirit . . . I believe that our work in the arts is more closely allied with

the larger continuities of religious belief and faith. The arts in this sense can be viewed as sacramental actions that symbolically represent the mysteries and intensities of inner experience . . . this kinship with religious ritual explains much of their potency. (1981, pp. xvi–xxii.)

Ironically, in some societies, particularly those that are impoverished, disease, either physical or mental, represents a threat to the entire community. According to Frank and Frank:

> The invalid is in conflict internally and is out of harmony with the group. The group must choose between abandoning the ill member by completing the process of extrusion or making strenuous efforts to promote healing and restore the person to useful community membership. (1991, p. 90)

In healing these afflicted souls, some societies in fact use healing rituals to invoke the spirit and extricate evil forces residing within the person. Other forms of traditional healing embrace a comprehensive relationship between healer-shaman and patient, a procedure akin to long-term psychotherapy. In those ceremonies that require confession, atonement, forgiveness, or penance, the achievement of worth is especially evident. The remedy of confession for cure suggests a parallel link between illness and transgression. Indeed, impersonal forms of confession and repentance, as in some Christian ceremonies, function as a purification process. As well so too does the process of other rites such as baptism, receiving of the sacraments, and the *mikveh*. Equally important to these events is the requirement of witnesses or community participation. This again suggests the necessity behind the faith community.

In discussing what practice (purification and enlightenment) is *not* in the book, *Every Day Zen: Love and Work,* Beck (1989) asserts that there are only two kinds of ways that things can go awry in our lives: one way is external events and the other way is internal events, such as physical illness. Rather than rely on religiomagical healing or shamans, Zen Buddhists depend on the practice of sitting in meditation. Although the solution sounds relatively simplistic, practice is horrendously difficult. Beck agrees that the sitting practice of becoming aware of everything that enters one's life (whether external or internal) is an inordinately laborious task. Yet, the end result is life transformation. As Beck so clearly states: "A mind that is not aware will produce illness" (p. 28). This truism eloquently points out that whether by shaman, priest, rabbi, minister, guru, et al., the ultimate passageway to mental health lies dormant within ourselves. In contemplating this, I wonder, can we exist outside community? No matter how meditative or spiritual we are, can we survive without this reinforcement of our reality? Is the reflective life of the hermit the ultimate spiritual existence? Perhaps the task for both patient and therapist is discovering the path that spiritually releases passageway toward mental health.

Spiritual healing is a spiritual re-birth, through which we enter into a fuller understanding. When all self-effort has ceased, then the miracle of healing takes place, swiftly and silently. Healing is a gift from God. We must become receptive to it. It is not because we are good enough, but because God is good enough to give it. (Price, 1983, p. 17)

But is the seeking of the spirit truly a passive process as suggested by Price or in fact a lifelong, active process? Does God approach us or do we approach God?

The question is, are we brave enough to tap in? And, if we are, how deeply are we willing to plunge? Authenticity lies within our innermost resources; it is an archaic life force that pervades our inner being and exists solely for the purpose of being awakened, revitalized, and released. Humankind's ever-present struggle with life's meaning is really within our grasp. We need only reach within in order to transcend and stay the course. As the old adage goes, "Bottoms up!"

# Chapter 3

# THE BELIEF ART THERAPY ASSESSMENT: INTERVIEW AND EVALUATION

"Man has no body distinct from his soul."

–William Blake

## INITIAL STAGES

The preliminary Belief Art Therapy Assessment (BATA) was developed *before* I initiated any research on the subject of mental health, spirituality, and its relationship to art therapy. Perhaps that was best. For what I discovered was that the research not only supported my thinking but also called out for such a battery to be developed:

> At this time there is no known objective measure of spiritual development. Most existing assessment is based on the clinical interview, including some history gathering, and interactions with the client. (Chandler et al., 1992, p. 171)

Additionally, Worthington (1986) recommended assessing the client to include his religious context and the importance of religion in his life. He suggested comparing the spiritual developmental level to other aspects of functioning to ascertain whether or not the client's religion was related to the diagnosis or etiology of the problem.

While the BATA is subjective since the administrant brings to the task his own talents, gifts, background, and feelings, the artwork contains an objective component. The investigation appears to be a cross between a heuristic study (which involves a phenomenological approach with an "introspective orientation toward the investigator's own consciousness") and a hermeneutic study ("which attempts to make sense of the "dialogical process between the inquirer and the data, texts or artifacts") (Junge & Linesch, 1993, p. 64). Although the data could be analyzed, categorized, and converted into mathematical computations, my precise desire was to create a battery that recognized the spiritual dimension of a person and contributed pertinent information in order to effect treatment.

The findings procured through the BATA can alter the therapist's direction so that he might incorporate a spiritual component from the *onset* of treatment and operate from a holistic framework that embodies the spiritual dimension of wellness as outlined by Hettler (1979, 1991).

Additionally, I have found that when armed with sufficient data, the course of treatment can be more efficiently expedited. In today's plagued economy, brief therapy is always preferable but more importantly, frugality of treatment (when applicable) is also encouraged both from a psychodynamic and family systems perspective. In fact, I ardently maintain that families can be instructed how to care for themselves within a brief timeframe. The argument stems from the fact that they have been caring for themselves all along, even when doing it badly. All the more reason to tap into a client's belief system; for in doing so, the therapist can empower the identified patient yet align with the hierarchic powers.

## THE DESIGN

The Belief Art Therapy Assessment (BATA) grew out of my conviction that people's belief systems were indigenous to their operational and systems functioning. Yet when I read Coles' treatise, *The Spiritual Life of Children* (1990), I thought his idea of asking children to "draw a picture of God" was intriguing, however, incomplete. Primarily, the idea of requesting children to draw an image of God, could be perceived as offensive to Judaic teaching as written in the Bible. It is stated that to create a graven image of God is in fact against Judaic instruction:

> Thou shalt not make unto thee any graven image, or any likeness *of anything* that *is* in heaven above; or that is in the earth beneath, or that is in the water under the earth. (Exodus, 1985, 20: 4)

Moreover, the commentary and interpretation of this commandment by Hertz compounds the consequences of such action since this is strictly forbidden. Such piety is also shared by other religions including the Moslems:

> *a graven image.* This verse forbids the worship of the one God in the wrong way. Judaism alone, from the very beginning taught that God was a spirit; and made it an unpardonable sin to worship God under any external form that human hands can fashion. No doubt His law hindered the free development of plastic

arts in Israel; but it was of incalculable importance for the purity of the conception of God. (Hertz, 5751 or 1990, p. 295)

Therefore, conducting such a task that could include a Jewish population or Moslem population required alteration. What I wanted to determine was what one *believed* in and how that creed impacted a patient's spirituality, family functioning, and ethical practice. I realized that the directive would have to be transformed in order to authenticate this information. Moreover, I found a mere two-dimensional drawing request limited in scope. The result was to not only redesign Cole's directive but also to include a multitude of two- and three-dimensional materials for all the obvious creative reasons.

Even more evident was the necessity for a preliminary interview to gather information about a person's past and current religious persuasion in order to rule out religiosity as a predictor of pathology. (Nevertheless, a review of the empirical literature on religious commitment and mental health confirmed that: "religion *is* associated with mental health benefits" (Gartner et al, 1991, p. 16).) However, this cannot always be confirmed by *real life* events. Yet, I felt that the interview process not only set the stage for the assessment but also contributed to the administrant's ability to spiritually connect with the client. Indeed, the ten rudimentary questions seemed to serve as springboards for more in-depth inquiry and discussion. (*N.B.: However, this depends on the sophistication of the inquirer but more importantly on the responsiveness of the patient.*) Thus, Assagioli's adage that one cannot help another past one's own level of development is particularly apt when confronting spiritual development (1989). The administrant should be reminded that his subjectivity and reaction is always present thus coloring and influencing the person being tested. To avoid this, one would have to be impersonal and robotic. Thus, the findings will always be contaminated by the administrant's posture.)

Furthermore, when conducting the BATA, I continue to encounter an unexpected phenomenon—the secondary gain of my own spiritual growth and development. This occurs simply by being in the presence of another human being and encouraging him to answer such questions as "What gives you strength and meaning in your life?" It does not matter if the person is emotionally disturbed, physically challenged, an atheist, an agnostic, a member of the clergy, or an ordinary layperson. The gift of being in another person's presence, openly searching for the meaning of life, and discussing one's relationship or nonrelationship with God is not only instructional but also strangely comforting. No matter what a person's degree of pain or pathology, it is truly illuminating to connect on such sacred ground. For after all, we are what we believe in and what we allow ourselves to become. Nothing more. Nothing less.

I must add that I believe in God as a ***spiritual element*** that ***animates*** the life force of every living being and thing. I also know that for most, this life form is choked and pushed so far down within our darkest fears, that we rarely allow its existence to surface. Perhaps invading this passageway can allow both clinician and patient to transcend this darkness and walk into light.

As Henry James once said, "We do what we can. We work in the dark. Our doubt is our passion. And our passion is our task. The rest is the madness of art."

## SUGGESTED ART MATERIALS TO HAVE ON HAND

### *Two-Dimensional Drafting Media*

Drawing Pencils (specifically No.1), Mars Staetler eraser, gum eraser, colored drawing pencils (minimum set of 12 colors), craypas (minimum set of 12 colors), pastels (minimum set of 12 colors), ink pens, colored markers (fine and broad nibbed, minimum set of 8 colors), crayons (minimum set of 16 colors, both large and small sized).

### *Two-Dimensional Painting Media*

Tempera paint (offering white, yellow, red, ultramarine blue, turquoise, and black *only*), watercolor (pan) cakes (same colors), acrylic or oil paint, and varied sized brushes.

### *Three-Dimensional Media*

Glue or glue sticks, scissors, clay, plasticene (preferably white or grey only), cardboard (various sizes), scrap wood, sculptamold, plaster.

### *Types of Paper*

Minimum: All sizes from 8.5″ x 11″ to 24″ x 36″, white, manila, and if possible, colored construction paper assorted (minimum 8.5″ x 11″ and 12″ x 18″).

*(N.B: The above are suggested materials to enhance creative expression, but often-times subjects introduce new materials not outlined on this list, e.g., microcrystaline beeswax.)*

## THE BELIEF ART THERAPY ASSESSMENT

# History Taking*

Name, Age, Religion, and Career (if applicable)

## *Questions*

1. What is you religious affiliation?
2. Have there ever been any changes in your religious affiliation?
3. When did these changes take place (if applicable) and what were the circumstances that caused this change?
4. Are you presently involved with your church, temple, or faith community?
5. What is your relationship with your pastor, minister, rabbi, shaman, or guru (state as applicable to interviewee)?
6. Do you have any religious/cultural practices that you find particularly meaningful?
7. What kind of relationship do you have with God, if applicable?
8. What gives you special strength and meaning in your life?
9. Is God involved in your problems? (Depending on how this is answered, you might want to clarify whether or not the subject involves God in his or her problems and/or blames God for his or her problems.)
10. Have you ever had a feeling of forgiveness from God?

*(N.B.: All of these questions need not be asked and also depending on personality and psychological parameters, one may choose to skip this section altogether since it may exacerbate psychosis.)*

**FIRST DIRECTIVE**

Please remember that the manner in which a subject is presented with the request to delineate his or her belief system is all-important. One could begin the topic by stating something like:

**Have you ever thought about how the universe was created and who or what was responsible for its creation?**

---

* (Based on Dombeck and Karl's (1987) Guidelines for Religious Interview)

Then once a dialogue regarding the topic is started, the administrant could actually lead into the art task itself by stating:

***Many people have a belief in God; if you also have a belief in God, would you draw, paint, or sculpt what God means to you.***

The former instruction should be stated exactly as it is written above since any deviation from the original intent might imply subject bias. The reason for the words ***"means to you"*** is essential. The author is not looking for direct representation (since this may be offensive in some religious / cultural background).

If a prospective subject is an atheist or agnostic, the inquirer might simply request that the subject attempt to delineate what it is ***he or she believes in***. If the subject believes in *nothing,* one could ask the subject to define that in the media. However, if the subject defines himself as an *agnostic* or an *atheist,* one might ask:

***Have you ever believed in God?***

If the answer is yes, one might then inquire:

***What caused you to no longer believe in God and when did that occur?***

(One could still ask questions 5, 6, 8, and 10 as stated above)

## POST-ASSESSMENT INTERROGATION

1. Could you explain what you have made and what that means to you?
2. Have you ever witnessed or seen God as you have delineated your art-work?
3. How do you feel about what you have just made?

Moreover, let the subject talk freely about his work and record significant verbal associates to the work produced.

*(N.B.: When questioning an atheist, question #2 in the post-assessment interrogation can be eliminated or altered to fit the specific confines of the subject's previous responses as derived from the interview format. For example: Have you ever derived strength and meaning as you created it in your art response?)*

## SECOND DIRECTIVE

Some people create the opposite of God simultaneously with the above directive of creating what God means to them. If, however, the subject does not, then state:

*Some people believe that there is an opposite of God. If you believe there is an opposite force, could you also draw, paint or sculpt the meaning of that?*

Naturally the same post-assessment interrogation can proceed following the latter request.

*(N.B.: Again, when conducting the second directive with an atheist, one might suggest that the subject delineate the **opposite** of what it is he or she believes in or derives meaning from in life.)*


## CONSIDERATIONS AND GUIDELINES FOR EVALUATIONS

### Administrant's Posture While Artwork Is in Process

If possible, the inquirer should remain silent and observant during the art process and not interfere with the artistic process. When the artwork is completed, the art therapist may offer comments, support, or active help when appropriate.

### Assessing the Artwork

The chronological age of the subject must always be considered when evaluating the artwork. Both art process and art product should be observed and duly noted when considering evaluation. Additionally, artwork in one medium will sometimes complement or contradict findings in another medium. It is important to note any unevenness of performance or sequence of work. Like all artwork, the BATA can be scored cognitively according to Lowenfeld and Brittain (1975). Thus a developmental stage and approximate age range of cognitive level of functioning can be assigned to the art response. (For example, the scribble stage, age 4–7 years, could be relegated to a piece of artwork that approximates this level of functioning.) Thus, the battery offers the administrant a snapshot of the patient's developmental level, affording the clinician a baseline from which to operate. Although one can evaluate the artwork and relegate a developmental stage to the product, in discussing this design with colleagues it became abundantly clear that assigning a developmental score contradicts the notion of utilizing the artwork as a way to embrace a client's spiritual need. In the words of one colleague, Elyse Capell: any attempt to "concretely score and categorize an abstract relationship seems to in fact de-spiritualize and demystify the nature of God" (personal conversation). Instead, the BATA expands on the principle of abstraction and offers the clinician the additional opportunity of tapping into the patient's spiritual belief system. Yet, if one wants to pay attention to the cognitive information, it is wholly possible that a cognitive delay might represent the arrestment of spiritual development (see Table 1, Appendix). Consequently, this information cannot be ignored. However, the stages of faith as outlined by Fowler (1981) will be examined in Chapter 4 to offer the reader a way in which to assess a person's spiritual level of development.

## Locus of Observation

In looking at the "formal qualities" of the artwork, the following areas should be considered: (These concepts are borrowed from Edith Kramer's outline of the developmental stages of art (1975)):

1. No product—withdrawal, playful experimentation, destructive behavior, extreme duress or anxiety due to nature of topic, resistance.

2. Product in the service of the defense—personal stereotype, repetition compulsion, banal commonplace product, bizarre stereotype.

3. Product in the service of primitive discharge—chaotic, aggressive, obliterating or undoing the end product, possibly violent in theme or nature.

4. Formed expression—successful, evocative art product with inner consistency, "true art" or nearly successful product. It is also important to observe aborted attempts at formed expression. (Look at how it failed and when it failed – verbal associates to the product are extremely important at this point.)

## Formal Qualities of the Artwork

What was the result of the process and end product? Was it empty, commonplace, banal, personalized, stereotypic, dull, original, creative, fragmented, integrated, static, in motion, rigid, fluid, frantic, bizarre, et cetera? Was form subordinate to color or vice versa? Did the subject exhibit skill or talent that might place him at an adult stage of development or artistic stage of development?

## Subject Matter

What themes emerged and were there any blatant contradictions between overtly stated subject matter and the message conveyed by the artwork itself?

## Attitude

1. Was the subject withdrawn, cooperative, suspicious, hypervigilant or paranoid, rebellious, anxious, charming? What was the person's temperament

as seen in the art session? Was he or she exuberant, overwhelmed by anxiety or the materials presented? What was the subject's activity level—hyperactive, deliberate, reflective, withdrawn, adaptive, constructive? Was he or she highly invested towards his or her artwork or indifferent? Did the artist seem proud or ashamed and self-denigrating or destructive?

2. How did he or she respond to the specific media chosen? Did he or she express any preferences or avoidance of specific materials offered?

3. Did any learning take place? Did the art activity contribute to expression of material not otherwise available? Could continued exploration of the art materials foster ego strength, ego gratification, ego maturation, and/or spiritual development? Was there capacity for other gratifications—not necessarily art, but perhaps playful manipulation of the materials?

4. What was the subject's sense of reality? Did he or she seem depersonalized or did he or she dissociate from the artwork? Were there distortions of self and/or body parts? What was the subject's perception of himself/herself in relation to others?

5. And what were the outstanding developmental capacities and strengths, deviations, visual motor functioning, and developmental stage as seen through the artwork? If there were pronounced deficits, were they constitutional and/or emotional or cultural?

Incorporating these aforementioned parameters should aid the practitioner in establishing a baseline for treatment and spiritual inclusion and/or development. Further examination of the stages of faith (as described in the next chapter) will assist the clinician in establishing a developmental baseline for both comparative and developmental purposes. *For comparative purpose, Table 1 can be found in the Appendix. This table compares various clinical theories. As well, the entire BATA is printed in Table 2 for photocopying.*

# Chapter 4

# SPIRITUAL DEVELOPMENT, BELIEF SYSTEMS, AND STAGES OF FAITH: IMPACT ON ASSESSMENT AND TREATMENT

and only God, omnipotent indeed, knew they were mammals
of a different breed.

—Mayakovsky

## TOWARD A BELIEF SYSTEM THEORY

In order to investigate the belief systems of both the clergy and lay populations, an area requiring examination is that of the stages of faith as outlined by James Fowler (1981). Fowler purports that like the normal developmental life cycles that humans traverse, so, too, are there equivalent developmental norms for the spiritual dimension. These stages are hinged on the works of Piaget (1969), Erikson (1963), Kohlberg (1969), and Levinson's (1978) stages and life cycles. In outlining these levels of faith, Fowler starts with Undifferentiated Faith, which occurs in infancy:

> In the pre-stage called Undifferentiated Faith the seeds of trust, courage, hope, and love are fused in an undifferentiated way and contend with sensed threats of abandonment, inconsistencies, and deprivations in an infant's environment . . . the quality of mutuality and the strength of trust, autonomy, hope and courage (or their opposites) developed in this phase underlie (or threaten to undermine) all that comes later in faith development. (1981, p. 121)

In accepting this premise, it is clear that the parental object imprints upon the infant not only the web of psychosocial mores but also the fund of basic trust which lays the foundation for a person's faith system or lack thereof.

Moreover, Fowler points out that the inherent danger or deficiency in this stage can operate in two directions: either an excessive narcissism dominates and distorts one's mutuality or extreme neglect or inconsistencies contribute to patterns of isolation and failed mutuality.

Fowler describes the next phase as "Stage 1, Intuitive-Projective." Developmentally, this generally occurs between the ages of three and seven. Imaginative processes are available and uninhibited by logical thought. During this stage of self-awareness, the imagination has the ability to unify and "grasp the experience-world in powerful images . . . that register the child's intuitive understanding and feelings toward the ultimate conditions of existence" (1981, p. 134).

Nonetheless, the intrinsic liability arises "from the possible 'possession' of the child's imagination by unrestrained images of terror and destructiveness or from the witting or unwitting exploitation of her or his imagination in the reinforcement of taboos and moral or doctrinal expectations" (1981, p. 134).

Before one can transition into "Stage 2, Mythic-Literal Faith," concrete operational thinking (as outlined by Piaget) has to emerge. In addition, an affective resolution of the Oedipal stage and/or submersion of these feelings into the latency stage must also occur in order to decipher what is real from what is not.

Developmentally, this next stage occurs during a child's school years, although this arrangement sometimes dominates in both adolescents and adults. During this period, the person begins to accept the stories, beliefs, and observances that are sanctioned by himself or his community. According to Fowler, beliefs are "appropriated with literal interpretations, as are moral rules and attitudes" (1981, p. 149). However, during this stage the child is incapable of stepping back and formulating introspective, conceptual meanings. Alas, this aforementioned limitation can result in an overcontrolling, perfectionism work ethic or in its opposite, the embrace of immorality because of past mistreatment, neglect, or the unmistakable aversion of significant others and/or community members.

Contradictions to the moral fabric of a community's stories, culture, and ritual, combined with reflection on those meanings, contribute to a transition into the next stage, "Stage 3, Synthetic-Conventional Faith." This transition into formal operational thought (as outlined by Piaget) makes such observation feasible and inevitable. It is in this stage that a person's world finally extends beyond the family. According to Fowler, at this stage, "faith must synthesize values and information; it must provide a basis for identity and outlook" (1981, p. 172). Although, developmentally, this generally occurs during adolescence, for some adults it becomes a perpetual place of equipoise and thus structures the quintessential environment in interpersonal conviction. Differences of others are viewed as differences in "kind" of person. Thus, the forming of a personal myth dawns: "the myth of one's own becoming in identity and faith, incorporating one's past and anticipated future in an image of the ultimate environment unified by characteristic of personality" (1981, p. 173).

As in previous stages, there are also potential pitfalls in the Synthetic-Conventional Stage. Primarily, expectations and judgments of others can become internalized and idolized. Later, this could impact one's autonomous judgment. Furthermore, interpersonal betrayals could lead to depression and despair "about a personal principle of ultimate being or to a compensatory intimacy with God unrelated to mundane relationships" (1981, p. 173).

Stage 3 is also subject to breakdown due to the following factors: contradiction between significant authority figures, marked changes by officially endorsed leaders, or changed policies and procedures previously held sacrosanct. Such encounters may lead to critical reflection on how one's beliefs and values have formed and changed and thus promote increased self-examination. Such contemplation can influence and encourage projection into Fowler's next stage of development, Stage 4, Individuative-Reflective Faith.

Movement from Stage 3 to Stage 4 is a critical transition hallmarked by the movement from late adolescence into adulthood. Unavoidable tensions arise during this phase. Primarily, accountability and responsibility for one's lifestyle, commitments, attitudes and beliefs are prevalent factors in determining a person's readiness for passage into the Individuative-Reflective Stage. Objectivity and critical examination trade places with subjectivity. Individuality versus group membership vies for position. Additionally, self-actualization contends with service to and being for others. More importantly, questioning of the relative collides with the possibility of an absolute.

Developmentally, this stage occurs in young adulthood, but as stated before, many adults do not construct it and according to Fowler, many adults do not embark on this journey until their late thirties or early forties (1981, p. 182). Because others, no longer define this new identity per force, it forges a new meaning fashioned on the template of its own boundaries and inner connections as a worldview. The strength of this developmental stage is its potential for critical investigation (self) and world vision (philosophy). Yet, its vulnerability resides in its strength: the overabundant confidence of the self's reality may result in overassimilating the perspective of others into its own worldview.

Transition into Stage 5, Conjunctive Faith, is due to the restless inner voice that gnaws at the core of one's inner being. Vapid meanings of one's life purpose signal the need for change. Previously accepted stories, myths, traditions, and rituals may suddenly collapse and unbridle the solidity of one's previous faith. Disillusionment and the recognition that life is beyond our comprehension press one toward a "new dialectical and multileveled approach to life truth" (1981, p.183).

Stage 5, Conjunctive Faith, is marked disparagingly by Fowler as the stage, which he can neither communicate nor understand. Generally, this confusing state occurs before mid-life. According to Fowler: "What the previous stage struggled to clarify, in terms of the boundaries of the self and outlook, this stage now makes porous and permeable" (1981, p. 198). Inherent in this stage is the need to both reclaim and rework one's past, thus opening up the voices of a "deeper self." This results in a caviling recognition of one's social unconscious, impregnated into a self-system by way of exposure to a particular social class, ethnic group, religious upbringing, or the like. Thus, this plateau weaves opposites in mind and experience. The result is an openness that threatens the parameters of one's self-system and world outlook, often leading to religious revelation or spiritual evolution.

The strength of this stage is the ability to see powerful meanings within oneself (or one's group) while simultaneously recognizing its past shortcomings due to the manifest peculiarity of transcendent reality. Paradoxically, the ability to understand truth at this juncture compounds the danger of becoming passive, complacent, or cynically withdrawn. More importantly, this stage is imprisoned by its vision and imperative of an inclusive community of being (the human family), and its inability to transcend this vision into a world reality. Thus, Stage 6 results.

Stage 6, Universalizing Faith, involves overcoming this paradox. As Fowler suggests, this can be accomplished

> through a moral and ascetic actualization of the universalizing apprehensions. Heedless of the threats to self, to primary groups, and to the institutional arrangements of the present order that are involved, Stage 6 becomes a disciplined, activist incarnation . . . (the) feel for transcendent moral and religious actuality give . . . actions and words an extraordinarily and unpredictable quality. . . . It is little wonder that persons described by Stage 6 so frequently become martyrs for the vision they incarnate. (1981, p. 200)

However, in discussing the leaders of Stage 6, Fowler is quick to point out that characteristics of the aforementioned have often included the heinous memories of such places as Jonestown, Guyana and the Reverend Jim Jones. He clarifies his position by purporting that attention must instead be given to the "criteria of inclusiveness of community, of radical commitment to justice and love and of selfless passion of a transformed world, a world made over not in *their* images, but in accordance with an intentionality both divine and transcendent" (p. 201).

People who forge the pathway of Stage 6 have a special grace that makes them seem more lucid and more fully human than the rest of us. Their community is universal and they are also apart from any practical regard. Life is concomitantly loved and not possessive. As a result, these people are able to commune with persons at any other stage of faith and any other faith tradition. As Fowler states:

> The bearers of Stage 6 faith, whether they stand in the Jewish, Christian or other traditions, embody in radical ways this leaning into the future of God for all being . . . these persons kindle our imaginations in these ways because, in their generosity and authority, in their freedom and their costly love, they embody the promise and lure of our shared futurity . . . sending shockwaves . . . their trans-narcissistic love of human futurity account for their readiness to spend and be spent in making the Kingdom actual. (1981, p. 211)

These qualities are those of the most ascetic, revered individuals. Images that come to mind are that of Jesus Christ, Joan of Arc, the Blessed Mother, Mary, and all the saints, to mention a few. For by definition, saints belong to God and aspire to that membership. Although man and woman also are part of the Kingdom, it is quite clear that saints belong to God in every deed and action they fulfill. One wonders if these traits can actually be attained by the mass. Surely, if we were all capable of transcending into Stage 6, the world would be a very different place; in fact, by definition, it would be utopia. Because of the loftiness of such a vision, it seems impossible for the human condition with all its foibles to possibly transcend such a view. Yet, in Fowler's mind, hope, which gives rise to faith, creates the mindset to sojourn such a course. He states:

> *Faith,* rather than belief or religion, is the most fundamental category in the human quest for relation to transcendence. Faith, it appears, is generic, a universal feature of human living, recognizing similar everywhere despite the remarkable variety of forms and contents of religious practice and belief. (1981, p. 14)

If one can give rise to such faith, perhaps the human condition could be restored to its optimistic potential. The pinnacle development of one's spiritual evolution is aimed at this stay. The journey to cross into this plateau, however, is both arduous and ever-present to maintain. The human condition seems to resist this stage of faith and in fact continually struggles against it. Interest in heightening one's spiritual development is the seed which plants the traveler onto this fruitful trail.

Because of these obvious dichotomies in the human condition, it seemed necessary to look at the belief/faith systems of those whom we look toward for our various religious tenets: priests, shamans, rabbis, gurus, ministers, et cetera. And so the path of these ascetic individuals necessitated investigation in order to fully explore and understand the lay people's condition within this context.

## TESTING THE CLERGY

When I first began this pilgrimage, it seemed obvious to examine the tenets of the clergy and those who ministered their religious and/or spiritual community toward a concept of health, well-being, and transcendence. In fact, because of the serious nature of these apostles, I mused (sometimes out loud) about whether or not their responses both on interview and via the art product would be dramatically different from the lay population. However misguided my notions, one priest, Father Joe, set me straight by affirming that in fact "priests (were) no closer to God than the average person." Somehow that surprised me. For whatever reasons implanted from my early childhood upbringing (Stage 2, Mythical-Literal Faith), I managed to idolize and elevate such religious, community positions. This served as a humble reminder that one elevates to this spiritual and sacred realm not by community definition but by God's. And rightly so.

## THE INTERVIEWS

By definition, clergy are not like lay people. Even though they may be no closer to God, in interviewing these individuals, I can safely conclude that as a group, they definitely think and operate somewhat differently than the average person. Their job description perforce demands such differences. And ethically, they are bound to uphold these principles by the religious doctrines, which in fact guide them. As a result, the interviews were remarkably long, in-depth conversations, which led to candid exploration of some of their innermost thoughts. To reprint all of the responses to each of the questions which I posed could, in fact, be a treatise all in itself.

Therefore, I will summarize and highlight the salient points of our conversations. In all, I tested three priests, three sisters, two Presbyterian ministers, two rabbis, two Episcopal ministers, a Unitarian minister, and a Baptist minister. Since the interviews alone required approximately two hours to complete, and an equal amount of time to transcribe, I limited my research to these few individuals. While certainly not a complete survey of the clergy, of interest was the overlapping ideas shared by these people regardless of their religious faith or background.

Although similar icons appeared in their responses when using the art materials, it would be unfair to suggest that any commonality had collective meaning or the like. Clearly, more investigation is warranted before any assumption can be made. The conversations which I had with the clergy, lay people, and patient population alike bore one common thread: I received a secondary gain (spiritually) just by questioning these tenets and being in the company of people who were willing to dialogue about God and/or their belief system. Each time I was in the presence of a person who engaged honestly about his or her feelings, I felt spiritually connected to him or her on a very sacred ground.

## FATHER JOE

Father Joe is a sixty-three year old Roman Catholic priest of Irish descent. Although he ministers on weekends at a local parish, during the week he serves as the Director of the InterFaith Chapel at a prestigious university. As a result, he is particularly learned in many areas of other religious faiths and in fact is fluent in several languages, including Hebrew. He was quite willing to participate in this study, and after the one and a half hour interview had concluded, he made a few remarks that I found both intriguing and worthy of future consideration.

Because he is musically oriented, he commented that he could just as easily have responded to the directive to "conduct, play, or interpret musically what it is that God means to you." (Naturally, the same substitutions would hold for the second directive and/or if the person tested was agnostic or atheist.) This gave me pause. I had not thought about the possible substantive investigations by other creative art therapies; clearly now, I could imagine the possibilities. I thanked him for his remarkable insight but pointed out that I felt only equipped to orchestrate this via the medium with which I am most comfortable–art. Nevertheless, it awakened in me the possibility of utilizing the BATA with various disciplines.

Another comment that he made at the end of our meeting was how useful he felt this experience would be for a group retreat. Again, I marveled at the scope and magnitude of such fields. We dialogued for some time about how this might be conducted. He imagined interviewing the group as a whole in a sort of TQM (Total Quality Management) "round robin" approach. He next suggested that the group could go off separately to create their individual responses with the art materials and then reconvene for a group discussion. Although this appeared limited in its breadth because of the confinement of group inclusion, it certainly would be a useful tool for meditative contemplation and personal insight. Clearly, the BATA could be utilized for purposes, which I had neither intended nor designed. This in itself seemed a positive indication.

Father Joe's response to the first directive can be seen in Figure 4-1. A huge orange, yellow sun covers the surface of the largest paper which I had avail-

Figure 4-1. Fr. Joe's light.

able. When questioned how that meant God to him, he responded, "I think of God as light and warmth that I can turn to. Certainly you can get that from other people all around you but sometimes, if you can't get that from human contact, then you can get that from God."

Of interest was Father Joe's perspective of forgiveness. I asked him how he could absolve people who had committed heinous crimes such as Hitler's genocide and similar atrocities. His straightforward answer clarified my understanding of both confession and penance: "I have always felt that if someone truly wants to repent that yes he can be forgiven, but it is God's decision as to what to do with that person; I am only a mediator." It seemed more palatable to leave the final judgment up to God to either absolve or convict a

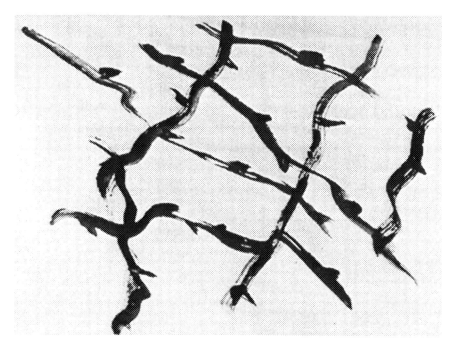

Figure 4-2. Fr. Joe's barbed wire.

person of his past sins. It answered some of the nagging questions raised by my patients who warred with these inconsistencies. And for me, it placed omnipotence where it rightfully belonged.

Naturally, I was curious about Father Joe's response to the second directive (to draw, paint, or sculpt the opposite meaning of God.) His decision to use the smallest paper which I had available seemed to underscore his need to contain these feelings. His comments, "I don't like to deal with that realm. . . . This isn't coming out right. I want to make thorns, a dead bush, but this looks like pussywillows . . . barbed wire, I guess," alluded to his obvious discomfort apparent not only in his banter but also in the speed with which he finished the task. While the prior directive necessitated approximately a half hour to complete, this second directive, Figure 4-2, was accomplished in just a few minutes.

When I questioned if he had ever witnessed the opposite of God as it was rendered and what that meant to him, he responded that he perceived God's opposite as "all that we have done wrong in our world—pollution, war, social injustice." Various other clergy whom I tested repeatedly uttered these thoughts.

The next priest whom I tested was unusually interesting in that he hailed from India. I suspected that his cultural background would greatly influence the responses to my questions. Remarkably enough, his cultural background had little to do with his retorts. Because his pronouncements were so obviously wise, I have chosen to reproduce his interview in its entirety.

## FATHER PAUL

Father Paul, age 33, was born in India to a Roman Catholic family. He was in the United States for an indefinite period of time for continued training. Because of the specific occupation that Father Paul had chosen, I decided to ask him when he first knew that he wanted to be a priest. Like Father Joe, Father Paul also knew by his high school years that this was to be his profession. He too had not felt a specific calling but his response to this query was as follows:

> **Fr. Paul:** No specific call—we normally believe it comes from testament or call from God. I never had such feeling . . . yet attraction to the church, the service that is being done . . . the other is the suffering of people and I had an attraction towards that—so that attraction was you are meant to realize that your field of work may be through this kind of service.
>
> **Ellen:** Have you ever changed your religious affiliation?
>
> **Fr. Paul:** Not as far as the service is concerned. But, this comes with your understanding of religion and your understanding of faith. There are always ups and downs with that. Faith is always something which you always question. You are not very sure of faith at any time. It always evolves so you question that.

Because of this response, I felt it necessary to springboard to the next few questions:

> **Ellen:** So you have questioned your own faith?
>
> **Fr. Paul:** Yeah sure.
>
> **Ellen:** Have you ever moved away from your relationship with God?
>
> **Fr. Paul:** I don't think so because I believe faith is not anything, which cannot be questioned. One has to have faith. You build it up on certain doubts, certain questionings and that is how your faith builds upon . . . maybe man has a certain capital or a certain belief that is given by the church or by the family, but that has to be personalized. You internalize that particular faith, what is given, and that I believe is then added to your own questionings. And doubts come and you try and understand your faith better and you

question it further. And, I think, through this questioning, through these doubts, your faith becomes stronger.

It seemed vividly clear that Fr. Paul was speaking of both Stage 5 and Stage 6 as outlined previously by Fowler. Again, this underscored the key differences in the thinking of such spiritual teachers. Although prejudice and discrimination seem to be heavily pronounced within our present society, people of this ilk seem to be immune from this thinking. Fr. Paul's answers, however, were remarkably candid and human; thus, his passionate outlook was both profound and infectious. At the time of the interview, he had only been in this country three weeks. Unfortunately for his parishioners, he had little direct involvement.

**Ellen:** What is your relationship with your pastor and community?

**Fr. Paul:** Back in India, I had certain people that I could go to. But then again, I like to solve my own problems; I believe that through questioning, through doubt. . . . I always try to answer my own doubt. So that has always made me self-sufficient. From that point of view, I go to myself. But not with practical problems; I go to others. But concerning faith, I just have my own values; maybe it's because of a certain experience I had in the beginning. . . . I had my certain doubts of the faith. . . . I never got a satisfactory answer.

**Ellen:** Can you share with me some of those doubts?

**Fr. Paul:** Studying philosophy, I had a doubt about the Trinity itself . . . three people in one person . . . it was a difficult concept to be digested. Your faith might be to disagree with that . . . or in your heart alone. Doubt really came to my mind. There was no reasoning of it. You couldn't really reason that out. I never found the answer except in faith . . . to fall back on your faith. But I still had my doubts persisting. It was a difficult time for me. But then since it was told to me, I got my answer in philosophy. During the course of time it is not really reasoning alone that is the answer to all your beliefs. Religion is not merely your reason, but also your emotions and perhaps something which is given to you as a faith . . . a capital . . . and you understand it only as you go by it . . . a way of touch and feel which you can not reason. It is something, which my mind cannot grasp. My mind perhaps is not sufficient to do that. But then my heart can touch certainly the essence of religion. And the mind has a place and certainly the heart has a place too. That's where I try to understand that point of view. There are certain areas, which my mind cannot touch, my heart can touch; that shows the importance to my heart and to my religion.

**Ellen:** That's helpful for me to hear personally as I have struggled with the trinity concept, too. Do you have any religious practices that you find meaningful?

**Fr. Paul:** I like certain things. Rituals are quite meaningful in their own way. Yet, when they become routine or mechanized they tend to lose meaning and all perspective. That system disturbs me. When there is nothing new that comes in or pertains to the time, the people or the culture, then religion can be meaningless. Of course, you fall back on your intuition and give strength and support to your practices. But I personally can find meaning (in the religious church practices) and make it more meaningful. You bring in your own personal meaning to this routine, this cycle, and so it becomes purposeful. I fashion it to the life of Christ and how he worked out certain struggles. Or through meditation, I can look at where I stand between the world and dogma.

**Ellen:** What kind of relationship do you have with God?

**Fr. Paul:** I cannot really say if it is deep or shallow. But I do have a relationship with God. I really believe that God is someone who really guides our actions without our knowledge. He is there for perhaps when we are not able to see or touch. And we never know that his presence is there. But yet there are certain things—chance opportunities, coincidences that you cannot explain, my coming here, for example. It just happened. And so there must be some sort of force that guides these actions so smoothly and applicable to you . . . a certain maybe a surprise which is in fact created by God Himself, I believe. He is working within. There may be something, perhaps, that makes people, for example, self-confident. Yet there is more than that, which cannot be explained, for all to grow.

**Ellen:** What gives you special strength and meaning in your life?

**Fr. Paul:** God is always there to give you strength and he gives us strength in our own selves—your own particular strength that you have in your self, your attitude coupled together with God's presence and your self-realization.

**Ellen:** Is God involved in your problems?

**Fr. Paul:** I shared with you this experience of coming here. I certainly had anxieties . . . where I would stay, what would happen and coming to an unknown land is always difficult. You always wonder. So there is a time you pray to God and you get it all worked out. His assistance was really fine. Otherwise, it would not have been possible.

**Ellen:** Do you ever feel God is responsible for your problems or get angry with God in anyway?

**Fr. Paul:** God plans everything. It would be easy to blame God, but if you see it from God's perspective, it is perhaps a stepping stone, a tragedy that has been planned for us to pass through, a juncture from which we try and catch up to Him. They (the junctures) make your life. So, from this point of view, I don't see them as problems but really as steps toward a movement in life. They have to be there, they are a part of life.

**Ellen:** Has there ever been a feeling of forgiveness from God?

**Fr. Paul:** God is forgiving. Whenever I go from him, he shows me there is certain planning in this. God forgives. I really believe that he forgives me. It is easier for me to reconcile that I am just a mediator for God. We cannot judge a person . . . a mental status . . . it is God's judgment. If a person is truly repentant, I trust him and God and then God is the one who forgives. And, I put them together. I can create that through a particular sacrament.

**Ellen:** How do you feel about murderous human beings when they say, "I am truly repentant?"

**Fr. Paul:** I am only a mediator. . . . I have no right to judge a person for that matter. God judges . . . We are never sure of that, whether it is right or wrong. A sin is sin. From our understanding we count it as a sin. From God's understanding, it may not be a sin. But if it is a sin, we may never know about it . . . and yet we cannot judge the person . . . perhaps because of this mental status. . . . I could never say that a person has really done something wrong. It is God that judges these things. I trust that when a person comes with a repentant heart, and he is truly sorry about what he has done and he feels that what he has done is a sin, I trust him and I trust God. And, I trust that He forgives the person. So I am just the mediator. . . . And God is the one that forgives so I put them together. That is the way I believe. So whoever comes to me with a repentant heart, I certainly believe that is reconciliation between God and him . . . and I can create that particular sacrament.

At this point, I turned to the art materials and quickly demonstrated how to use media with which Fr. Paul was unfamiliar. I then asked him to complete the first directive. Below are his responses as he worked toward that end.

**Fr. Paul:** This is a difficult concept . . . for me it is from within . . . I cannot see God as someone who is very far away. I can only see it from within and developing within the world. It's almost impossible for me to do it.

It appeared that the assignment was provoking much anxiety. He seemed inordinately indecisive about what material to use.

**Fr. Paul:** The medium is quite strange to me. It's not something that I am used to. It begins inside of me–my mind, my body. That's the concept overall.

**Ellen:** I wish I could help you. It's a very difficult task, I know.

**Fr. Paul:** It would be very easy for some to see God as a shepherd, but for me it begins some way from within but how do I do it? It keeps growing as days go by. This medium is difficult (paint).

**Ellen:** Did you like it as a child?

**Fr. Paul:** I gave it up as a child. The concept is very hard for me.

**Ellen:** It seems like you are struggling with rendering that feeling that is inside of you.

**Fr. Paul:** Can I put words on it?

**Ellen:** Yes. It makes you feel how?

**Fr. Paul:** I don't know.

**Ellen:** They probably should have given this to you in the seminary. (We both laugh.)

**Fr Paul:** This is supposed to be representing God and how man dominates and doesn't let God dominate. (N.B.: At this time he wrote the following, "The emergence of God and discover the unknown.")

**Fr. Paul:** The purple part and the red part are myself. Sometimes the purple part doesn't mingle with God and so perhaps the meaning of it is allowing the mingling of God to take over your whole being. The distinguishing of humanity that doesn't permit the mingling of God, my own self-interests, my own motives, those are times I keep God away.

**Ellen:** It's nice to know that even priests struggle with that.

**Fr. Paul:** The closer you are to God, the more you'll be tested the more that humanity comes to your mind and that is quite testing. So the struggle is always there. That struggle is possible to keep God away from you. You can't really sustain that struggle and realize that God is in there waiting.

## FAITH IN THE PRODUCT

Figure 4-3 is Fr. Paul's illustration of both what God means to him and the opposite force to God. He reiterated again that it is we who keep ourselves from mingling with God and that the potential for that force is in there all the

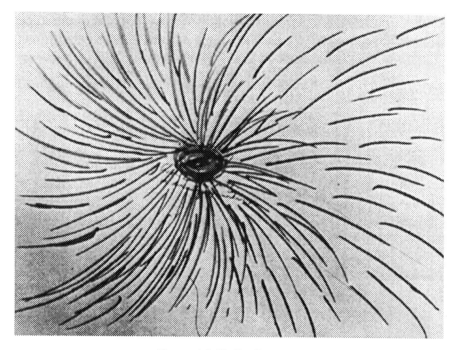

Figure 4-3. Fr. Paul's work.

time. He stated, "It begins within your own self. It begins inside. If the opposite force impacts you, it keeps God away from you."

In looking at Fr. Paul's artwork, an inner eye in the very central part of his drawing seems clearly evident. This vortex was created from the center out and as Wadeson suggests (1980), it may represent more volatile, labile emotions that are often seen in the drawings of bipolar depressive individuals. This is not to suggest that Fr. Paul was manic depressive but to accentuate the turbulence and force, which God has instilled within him. The radiant splendor of the red and purple lines may also illustrate the aggression and dominance which Fr. Paul's yields as God's power.

Furthermore, when assessing a person's spiritual development via Fowler's stages of faith, one can assign a stage of faith certainly by the verbal responses to both the interview and directives. In this case, clearly, Fr. Paul is operating at Stage 6, Universalizing Faith.

However, what about the client that is non-verbal? Is it possible to buttonhole his spiritual level of development based on his artwork alone? Or is it conceivable that perhaps his stage of artistic development as outlined by Lowenfeld and Brittain (1975) might in fact match Fowler's Stages of Faith so that one might be able to draw parallels in arrested cognitive delays and arrested spiritual development? Could there be corollaries? Clearly, these are questions that will remain unanswered until a sufficient body of data is compiled to explore these hypotheses. I urge the reader to ponder such inquiry and examine these postulates when utilizing the BATA and to note where there, in fact, might be matches between both cognitive and spiritual arrestment. My reasoning behind entertaining such discussion is that I have always concluded that cognitive development and emotional development have been uniformly arrested at the same levels. Moreover, as the patient improves in art therapy treatment, I have noted cognitive gains and emotional gains have occurred simultaneously (see Horovitz, 1981, 1983; Horovitz-Darby, 1987, 1988). Could this apply to spiritual development, too?

## SISTER MIRIAM

Sister Miriam, a Catholic nun, was 59 on interview. Besides ministering others, she functioned as an English professor at a nearby college. Again, I questioned whether or not she felt a specific calling in choosing her vocation:

**Sr. Miriam:** Well I entered the Novitiate when I finished high school and so I was rather young when I arrived at this decision. We used a word like vocation, which is in a sense a call. Somehow that always seemed so dramatic to me like God was calling and saying, "You hoo, hey Miriam." And I think it's more like any decision or choice you make about something that you want to do. For me, my mother was a teacher and my aunt was a nurse and so I always had this back and forth and I think part of my interest in becoming a teacher sort of connected me to the sisters.

In asking about any changes in her religious affiliation and when these changes occurred, Sister Miriam responded more in keeping with the changes attributed to Vatican II:

**Sr. Miriam:** Well, I think so much has happened in the last thirty years. . . . I guess sort of rolling with the changes represents rethinking of things. I certainly would never choose to go back to the older assumptions. I see a lot of that as people needing to preserve the past and I suppose that just doesn't appeal to me and also I suppose I think I have evolved in a lot of ways. Looking at ourselves and the Church very differently then we did in the 1940s, I think that's very healthy.

In asking about her relationship with a pastor or the community, she responded:

**Sr. Miriam:** My work is as a professional person in literature and a teacher. I am certainly involved with my parish. I like to do liturgical ministry. I feel that is something I can contribute. I would be interested in doing more things if time were not such a constraint. I guess I consider myself a member of certain local communities–the college and I like living in a parish. I moved from the college to a parish. A place opened up and I was one of the people who had put up for some space but one of the things that attracted me to that option was that I could live in the parish convent and be a part of that. It seems to me that there is something valuable about living with a cross-section of people.

In inquiring about any religious practices, which she found meaningful, she replied:

**Sr. Miriam:** Well, I think in the congregations. Office or liturgy of hours . . . that is an ancient, really a monastic tradition. I always found that very beautiful. Primarily it makes use of the psalms. Selected scripture readings. The liturgies or prayer services use psalms, but this is regular formulation–it takes you right through the year and all the liturgical seasons. It's an adaptation I think of what the sisters call the Divine office of what the priests used every day. But partly because its seasonal, there is a poetry about it–a kind of comprehensiveness about what is there and terms of human experience and life and reverence for God and I find that very beautiful. I try to take the Eucharistic ministries on a daily basis. And I guess personal prayer, quiet time, I find is very beneficial.

When asked about her relationship with God, Sr. Miriam responded:

**Sr. Miriam:** Well, I would say we are quite good friends. ***She's*** terrific. It's interesting as a child, I was brought up on these mysteries and truths and misunderstandings. I had a basic religious faith and went through these images of God with a book saying I got this on you. I suppose it's sort of like Santa Claus and the Easter Bunny that they use to threaten people. So I suppose I have some ideas about how people shouldn't present God or Santa Claus as a disciplinarian, a threat you know and all that. It seems to me that we have come to a kinder and gentler understanding of God. I suppose for anybody who is reflective, the issue really is looking around the world . . . there are all these unanswerable questions . . . a giant accident preventer. There are so many things that have touched me in my life and its not just accidental.

**Ellen:** You said "she," do you feel God is unisex?

**Sr. Miriam:** I guess I do find myself reacting to that when more attention has been paid to gender specific language. . . . You know, kind of patriarchal. . . . I go back to something in Plato when one half seems to seek the other . . . the concepts of yin and yang, I transfer that to the notion of God combining the best elements and I suppose I like to joke about it to get a rise out of people. And, often I adapt the language and edit it. I find that less abrasive somehow. There seems to be more latitude with the Holy Spirit. But I don't feel obliged to shout it out. . . . I feel it expresses my grasp of what that is all about.

I then inquired as to what gave Sr. Miriam special strength and meaning in her life.

**Sr. Miriam:** A lot of it has been people who have been important to me. People who have taught me or good friends, I suppose that kind of interaction that goes on. There are many things that I find myself reacting to things so much like my mother. But, I kind of enjoy it in a way; it makes her present again. Anyway, when you see people who are generous and committed and care about other people there is something there that causes you to go out on a risk. I am not altogether sure why some people become cynical, but just knowing that there are other people out there who gamble and shoot their wad. For me, it seems to me in great measure people who have been part of the fabric of my life and religious faith. I think there is some kind of underlying responsiveness that is just there.

At this point, Sr. Miriam became obviously saddened as tears welled up in her eyes. I offered her a tissue, and waited for a clue to go on. Somehow, I didn't feel quite comfortable broaching the subject of her discomfort and so I continued the interview when she regained composure and asked her if God was ever involved in her problems.

**Sr. Miriam:** I guess there could be various ways that I could interpret that. I don't think God creates our problems. I think we are pretty good at creating those for ourselves (chuckles). One of the things that I enjoyed was that my prayer of desperation was "Oh gee, God, just get me out of this one!" But I guess I remember being told that I tend to be a problem solver. I always try to figure out some possible solutions. This right idea doesn't surface out of anything I was cooking up. I realize that there is a psychological explanation for that . . . the creative subconscious and all that. . . . But, I suppose that I feel that comes from a connection with God. And I tend to say almost humorously that we tend to involve God (in those workings). The roughest thing I can remember going through was my uncle dying about fifteen years ago of cancer. . . . It wasn't some toxic attack on our family, and so it was not so much a blaming as a pain.

This seemed to lead to questioning her faith in God and whether or not she had ever turned away from God.

**Sr. Miriam:** I guess I could say as an ultimate answer no . . . which is certainly not to say that we haven't had our arguments (chuckles again). I guess I'm just trying to think in terms of how to sort that out. . . . I guess having described that experience about my uncle's death. You know certainly anger has to be a part of grief and sometimes we don't even recognize or identify them and I guess I may not have at that time and uh . . . my reactions were much more likely resolved by my family. That wasn't the way I had expected things to be. He was much younger than my mother and I thought that he would be around when my mother died to kind of hold us together and all that . . . and he wasn't going to be there . . . (she began to cry). Sorry and . . . so I suppose that kind of shock and sadness rather than anger and questioning and wondering. I can say rather humorously that I'm perfectly capable of creating my own problems . . . thank you very much (chuckles) and I really don't have to necessarily feel somehow that God is out to get me. And, perhaps maybe that's because so many of my experiences have been rescued from some of my own ways of getting myself into trouble. Maybe it's partly a Christian spirit. I do remember a very close friend died and being very angry at people who had not been properly supportive . . . but that's quite different.

**Ellen:** I see how close you felt towards your mother, you misted up when you spoke of her as well as your uncle. (When asked if she ever felt a feeling of forgiveness, she merely stated, "Absolutely.")

## The Art Task

She chose to work with paint and demonstrated a bit of anxiety about working with the materials since it had been so long. Some instruction alleviated the discomfort.

**Sr. Miriam:** The colors are so exciting to me . . . you do this on regular basis, Ellen?

**Ellen:** Yes. (I then explained a little about my work. We talked about a deceased, artistic nun, whom we both knew, and how unfortunate it was that I didn't get an opportunity to test her. This chitchat seemed to relax and encourage exploration of the art materials.)

**Sr. Miriam:** In recent years, we have been in a climate that allows credibility and respectability to the mystical and the transcendent. Post-war years, it was pretty scientific. To be otherwise, you were considered an oddity to be looking toward religious values. People would only put their trust in what you could see or trust and it just seems to me that the climate has changed. People like Scott Peck for instance . . . (starts referring to the picture) . . . this is supposed to be the light and the darkness. It sort of looks like a jellybean. This is supposed to be gold. (She goes back to the task.) I'm almost finished with this creation here. There is something about playing with these colors that's absolutely delightful. Well mostly what we have here are images of light . . . basically a daytime/nighttime. This was supposed to be a candle here or suggest a candle effect. This was supposed to be some significance about light in the darkness; that's what it's suppose to mean. The daytime here is kind of a water effect and grass and skies. The gold is sort of showering the person.

**Ellen:** When you talked about the light and the darkness is this an evil force or . . . ?

**Sr. Miriam:** I think this is meant to be the light and the darkness and perhaps its disproportionate since I got carried away with my colors . . . somewhere hidden in the darkness there is a glimmer of light. (I then asked about the opposite force.)

**Sr. Miriam:** (She chose a smaller paper and chit-chats again. She asked about Fr. Joe and what he chose and I explained that he had quite a similar response to hers. She seemed quite surprised.) This looks more like a sweet potato (chuckles). This part over here is the force of evil. I guess my idea was like the fallen angel . . . this figure was created to be glorious because this pocket of evil circulated whatever you call that emotion or passion . . . or something and then giving off all these incredible vibes and I kind of left this arrangement of this blue and black actually. It seemed dark enough, but it was a little bit deceptive in that it could be something energetic and glorious and I got myself backed off the page and the attempt at gold was to represent something about God and I guess the circle image, but it sort of got a bit of elongated here. But I guess we have both forces giving off vibes. And I got carried away with the good and evil. This is not to say that evil is more powerful then good. I guess I would have to redraw this on a bigger piece of paper (chuckles again). But anyway, what was

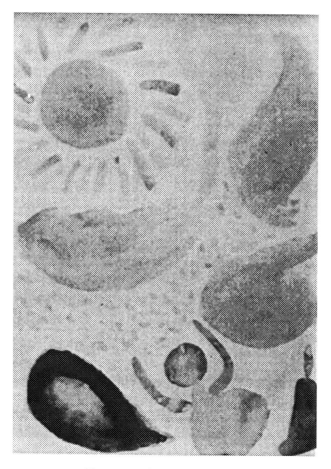

Figure 4-4. Sr. Miriam's work.

interesting about doing these was that I really was not starting out with a design. I just messed around with the paints and shapes and would see what they would be like on a paper. It's interesting to me because I'm used to being more verbal.

Again in looking at the artwork, here Sr. Miriam has combined both the forces of "good and evil" on the same page. Like Fr. Paul's response, she, too viewed them as residing within the same confines. Thematically, as I tested other theologians, I marked the repetition of this occurrence. I wondered silently whether or not this was in fact a common occurrence amongst people who wandered the halls of Universalizing Faith, Stage 6. Scratching my head at the similarities, I again speculated about these commonalities. No answers existed for such confounding questions, just more doubt. Again, I marveled at the possibilities and questioned the connection between artistic, developmental levels and possible spiritual developmental stages.

Continually, I kept coming back to Cathy Moon's poignant warning: analyzing the image removes the mystery and awe invoked by God's presence. Numbly, I internalized the possibility of treading on such sacred ground and contemplated whether or not on some level, the interpretation and analysis was perhaps blasphemous. But, this I believe again was connected to Stage 2, my mythical-literal teachings ingrained from my limited Judaic upbringing. Naturally, this led me to my next subject, Rabbi Mark.

## RABBI MARK

At the time of the interview, Rabbi Mark was 39 years old, and had grown up as a Reform Jew. He was currently practicing in a Reform congregation. Because of the questions that had surfaced from the previous interviews, I raised other subjects that I had not discussed with the aforementioned subjects.

For example, since there is no confession in the Jewish religion, I questioned to whom he divulged his concerns or questions. Unlike the concept of confession, he used the senior Rabbi and explained that there was no hierarchy. He clarified that the relationship was in fact more collegial. He further elucidated that this would be limited to congregational concerns and *not* personal issues or concerns.

Next, I asked him about his religious practices and if he derived strength and meaning from anything in particular. In addition to daily prayer, he talked about the Sabbath as meaningful and conducting his life in "aspects of sensibilities from what [he ate] to what [he wore] to social commitments." Dumbfounded by what he meant, naturally I asked him to expound and learned that he had been a vegetarian for the last twenty-one years, which grew out of his approach to kashrut, the Jewish system of eating. Because kashrut included "recognizing the sanctity of life," Rabbi Mark decided to give up meat, leather garments, or garb of any kind procured from a dead animal (e.g., pelts), and to use only soaps devoid of animal fat.

In inquiring about his relationship with God, he responded that his relationship was "personal . . . mystic by religious approach." In exploring what he meant by that, he clarified that in his daily prayer he included his desire for God to be nurtured and strengthened by his worship so that in turn he could then strengthen and nurture others. He went on to say that he was "concerned about God's life" and that he was "rooted in not only (his own) belief" but those "beyond the edge of rational explanation: non-rational explanation or experience . . . is very important to religious dimensions."

Naturally, I asked him to continue; he clarified:

**Rabbi Mark:** Irrational could be things that are mutually exclusive, you know like a square in a circle. In logical ways, there are things that are self-contradictory that I would say are irrational, as well as things that are wildly psychotic at the other end, different kinds of irrationality. But non-rational things are things, in logic, that we can't usually manipulate what the truth consists of and what the consequences are. But when you back up at a certain point, there are premises that you can't prove or disprove, you (merely) accept. These are based on experience; they are based on a variety of other things and some of them you accept on those non-rational levels. Some of them are emotional, some are experiential, and they are for good and bad reasons. I think our struggles with notions about evil are the down side and people rarely ask why does my spouse love me or why is that kid suffering and get any kind of understanding. They are both non-rational.

Like other clergy members, Rabbi Mark also concurred that he derived strength and meaning in his life from both his relationship with God and the sense of strength that it offered him as well as his relationships with people. From those two elements, he gained a "sense of centeredness." In discussing his problems and God's possible involvement in these constructs, Rabbi Mark discussed his feelings about doubt and exactly how that impacted his belief system.

**Rabbi Mark:** I think anyone who truly believes has moments of doubt. I think that belief without some evaluation and struggle with that belief is rather shallow. If I see horrendous things, I wonder how can this happen? Theologically, you can manipulate things, but that's not the whole of religion. It's not just theology . . . there are things that lead me to question. There are times when prayer is vacant and it doesn't connect. When I'm not playing my instrument well and am discordant, that leads to doubt and causes problems.

In asking him to clarify if in fact he then blamed God for his problems, like other theologians, he responded unequivocally that he did not. Instead, he, too, found the human condition at fault. He elaborated, "Human beings are mixed between our animal selves and metaphoric angelic selves, that quality essence like God. It's a tension . . . but I don't think God wants us to be God-like. I think He desires that we be fully human and sometimes that means we get involved in the muck and mire of what goes on in our world. We have to be involved in order to make (the world) a better place. If we are not involved in the mud, we can't fix it either." He further amplified, "I do feel that I get a particular strength from God to face the problems, particularly the worldly problems."

Unlike the responses from other Christian disciples, the concept of forgiveness from God was somewhat foreign to him. Although he associated forgiveness to rituals around specific holidays (e.g., Yom Kippur and Rosh Hashanah), he firmly believed that forgiveness from God was a direct result of "righting people whom we have harmed" as opposed to coming from a higher being. In thinking about the biblical teaching of the Old Testament, this reminded me of the old maxim, "an eye for an eye, a tooth for a tooth." In broaching this subject of atonement, I felt the need to inquire about his feelings regarding life after death. Since the Mythical-Literal Stage of Jewish doctrines contradicts this concept, I was curious as to how he judged this explanation. Although he alleged that there were some "Jewish speculations about what happens after (you) die," he found it inconsequential to how he lived. Instead, he reiterated the tenets, which I had been taught: one's memory on earth is perpetuated by the good deeds performed while alive.

Nevertheless, I inquired about the purpose behind the daily minyan service conducted for one year after a person dies. He simplified, "I guess that we have a sense that the spirit goes back to God." Having never heard that theory, I asked him to elaborate.

**Rabbi Mark:** There are theories of resurrection. The Christians got it from Judaism in some measure. But those were battles going on between Jews about speculative things that were in some ultimate way not terribly important to what we do as Jews in terms of our practice in our life. In the Bible, I could identify theories about life after death in a place called Sheol, which is all too often translated as Hell in Christian Bibles, but it is not Hell at all. It is just this place underneath earth, usually under mountains where dead people go and live in this other existence. There is no moral judgment attached to it. It's just where you go when you die. That was a theory early on. There is also Jewish folklore about heavenly things. There is not much folklore about places of punishment.

## The Art Task

In asking Rabbi Mark to do the first directive, I reiterated that I was not asking him to draw, paint, or sculpt a picture of God but instead to create what it was that God *meant* to him. Nevertheless, I wanted to make sure that

I was not offending him or asking him to make a graven image. Yet he stated that what I requested did in fact border on this gray area. He expounded, "I guess that is the prohibition against graven images or imaging God. It is just going to be (my) personal image of God and it's only at best a human eye view, never anything better. So I will try and draw something, an experience, a connection, a reframing rather of what God means to me per se."

What occurred next was *radically* different from anything that I had observed. Rabbi Mark began to creatively use colored construction paper in a three dimensional construct. He asked for items, which I had not brought. (I since have added the following items to my repertoire of available materials: scissors; glue; gold, silver, and copper markers; glitter; and cardboard.) Fortunately, he had these items in his desk drawer. (N.B.: The confines of testing people in their environment as opposed to my studio certainly has limited my choice of materials. Nevertheless, when working within my office studio, I offer any art materials which I have on hand and I would strongly urge the reader to do the same.)

Rabbi Mark was utterly consumed by this project and worked for approximately one hour in silence. He created a beautiful sculpture, which can be interpreted from several different perspectives (see Figures 4-5 and 4-6). Moreover, while creating this work, it began to thunder and lightning. We both laughed with the implicit fear that perhaps we truly were bordering on angering God by forming a graven image.

I was quite literally struck by the beauty of his finished creation. I inquired as to whether or not he practiced art outside of the office. I was surprised to learn that in fact he did not but instead, he cooked. He then said, "You know, it's interesting, very interesting. An image that runs through my mind is a description of Sinai . . . one of them is that in the Hebrew context it says, 'And they saw thunder and lightning.' It didn't say heard so it leads me to think something awesome happened to our ancestors beyond the normal sensory description and I'm waiting to see it."

He went on and further described his feelings connected to the piece:

**Rabbi Mark:** I guess by some measure it should be aesthetically pleasing. My relationship with God should be in some sense. I needed to create something that had a sense of dynamism to it that changed, that wasn't static because I don't think my relationship with God is static. Since I am mystic, another way I describe my relationship with God is as phenomenology of relationship. I learn about my relationship with God from my relationships with people. That can't be static; it has to be dynamic. It has to have quality change to it, open development, as I grow and as God grows. That happens in relationships. In some measure, using all the senses, I tried to depict something that was representative of these senses.

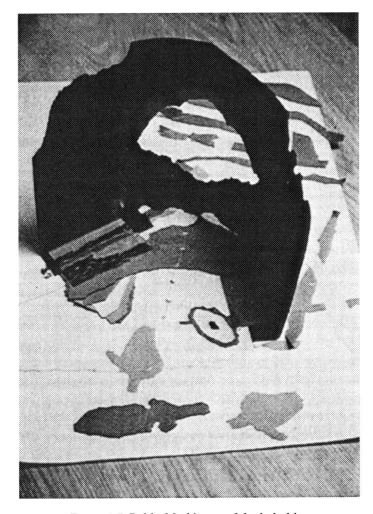

Figure 4-5. Rabbi Mark's eye of the beholder.

Visual is easy. Here, one looks through an eye and one gets a sense of an eye looking back at us. The shapes that I tore in the beginning served as the base of an ear, which leads to a representation of measured sound. Hearing is very different. It has a much more environmental quality about it than focus quality. I specifically made mitten hands because I wanted them to be clumsy. I think we are clumsy about this stuff. And then I attached a tongue and a nose.

Everyone focuses on what Moses saw with the burning bush, how long it takes to see a bush burn and be unconsumed. . . . I was wondering what the bush smelled like that was burning but not consumed and how that would smell very different from wood smoke. It would have to. I hadn't

Figure 4-6. Rabbi Mark's eye of the beholder (view 2).

thought about that until I was engaged in this either. . . . This opens us up in different ways.

I made the big eyes so different things could be seen and I curved it because I think that's how we see things. We very rarely see things straight and I used the rainbow colors because the whole spectrum is included, including black and white. I put the gold beading going under and over. I think that's part of the mystery—that the lines don't connect.

I guess my real first spiritual experience where I really was getting through with God was when I was fifteen and part of what happened was visual as well as what went on inside. It included beaded light. It was not quite gold, it had more of a copper color to it. Anyway, I was praying. I had spent the morning studying and some section of the Talmud said, "I set before you life and death, a blessing and a curse. Choose to be where you live. It is not too far off. You have to go up to the mountain to bring it back. It is right here and you can do it."

And, I had this incredible, timeless experience. I had no sense of time or how long it lasted. I got a feeling inside of me like this overwhelming physical rush, adrenalin running, hyper [activity] as well all mixed together. I perceived this visual thing of light and a skewed eye coming into the room, all directions in the room. I wouldn't say there was any source to it. The light was not in me; it was outside. But, the feeling was in me. . . . That was around the time I started thinking of becoming a rabbi.

At this juncture, I asked Rabbi Mark if he had ever witnessed God as he had created this work and he said, "Well, yes, this first experience, but I don't think this is a totality. I wouldn't call it a meeting ground really. I don't feel comfortable with the notion of meeting God because I guess I get a sense that we can bear witness before God and we can bear witness to human beings about God, but witnessing God gives me a sense of capturing God, which I don't think I can do. I don't think human beings can do it. It's just way beyond us."

Additionally, Rabbi Mark stated that he didn't believe in an opposite force to God since it bordered on an "agnostic position. If there were an opposite force, it would be, in fact, *still* a creation of God."

In viewing the artwork of Figures 4-5 and 4-6, black and white photography cannot bear justice to its splendor. In fact, in contemplating this work, both during the process and in its state of completion, I experienced what I believe was an archetypal, primordial response, akin to past musical experiences that have electrified and physically charged my senses. This is truly what Kramer meant when attempting to articulate the wonder and mystery associated with "true art or formed expression." If ever I had seen a Stage 6, Universalizing Faith, artistic level of development, by George, this was it. As Joseph Campbell once stated:

> It is the artist who really finds the images that are poetic, human and universal. That's what mythology is all about: it's poetry rather than prose. Art and myth are metaphors simply because they must deal with the ineffable, and the only way human beings can do that is through the use of symbols and poetic images that express things that are otherwise inexpressible. . . . To look at art without a sense of poetry , without a capacity for metaphor, leaves us with nothing but dead objects which decorate our walls. (source unknown)

Harding transcended this concept in her treatise on *Woman's Mysteries*. About the archetype she stated, "Whenever the archetype clothes itself with adequate symbols . . . it takes hold of the individual in a startling way, creating a condition of being deeply moved, the consequence of which may be immeasurable" (1971, p. x). Jung also bellowed about the power of the collective unconscious and how it impacted our perception of the world:

> The impact of the archetype whether it takes the form of an immediate experience or is expressed through the spoken word, stirs us because it summons up a voice that is stronger than our own. Whoever speaks in primordial images speaks with a thousand voices; he enthralls and overpowers, while at the same time he lifts the idea he is seeking to express out of the occasional and the transitory into the realms of the ever-enduring. (1966, p. 129)

But, secretly I wondered, who is capable of judging such a concept? And should this even be weighed? Should one attach spiritual development or arrestment to a stage of artistic development? What greater purpose could it serve? Did this border on "imagicide" (Moon, 1990)? Could stages of faith be classified via stages of artistic development?

There really didn't seem to be answers to these questions, just more doubts. But somewhere in my arsenal of tricks, I was certain of one thing: These questions which I posed coupled with the resulting artwork offered new insights into a person's spiritual psyche and offered a new dimension from which to operate and transcend.

Although I could continue with multiple transcripts of clergy members that I have tested, these four illustrations seem to epitomize the types of responses that I obtained. Although the artwork was varied both in its artistic and developmental elements, the verbal responses to the questions that I posed seemed remarkably similar. If nothing else, it offered credence to Fowler's stages of faith and hypothesis about spiritual development and dimension.

Since artwork is also individually tailored to the perceptions, abilities, and experiences of the individual, I suspected that the variations would be quite dissimilar. Yet, the verbal associates attached to the art product offered clarification and insight into the person's creative repertoire when investigating the hallmarks of the spiritual dimension. I was able to conclude that in using this assessment, a clinician could extract beneficial information that identified the spiritual dimensions of a person and in fact mapped out a blueprint from which to operate when wandering the halls of the spiritual psyche and soul.

# Chapter 5

# THE BELIEF ART THERAPY ASSESSMENT CONDUCTED ON ADULT ARTISTS

> We remain, as children, unaware that our languages, verbal and visual, through which we acquire and present information are symbol systems. We do not realize that they are inventions by means of which we communicate.
>
> –Miriam Lindstrom (1957)

Creativity is both a gift as well as a curse. Although most wish for such divine inspiration those who possess this faculty, often vilify its power. For creativity's gift often carries the added dimension of harboring the collective spirit of humankind. Burdened with that responsibility, a creative person has little to no control over his or her own life. Instead, the message orator is not free but instead captive and driven by this trust. Thus, the artist may be destined to walk the corridors that have plagued the tortured souls of time.

> Art is a kind of innate drive, which seizes a human being and makes him his instrument. The artist is not a person endowed with free will who seeks his own ends, but one who allows art to realize its purpose through him. As a human being he nay have moods and a will to and personal aim, but as an artist he is "man" in a higher sense–he is "collective man," a vehicle and molder of the unconscious psychic life of mankind. (Jung, Vol. 15, 1966, par. 157)

This work that artists do may be peaceful, blissful and at once harmonious. As well, it can be dark, agitated, and filled with the horrors of anger, rage, and discontent. Wadeson (1990), Marano Geiser (1990), Ramseyer (1990), and McNiff (1992) have openly discussed our need to embrace our dark sides in order to resonate with the patient.

Wadeson (1990) emphasizes the necessity of working with patients in an "emotionally, non-exploitive, clinically responsive way" in order to promote self-awareness (p. 110). She also urges the art therapist to recognize his or her voyeurism and adopt his or her demons. In doing so, one not only reverberates with the patient's issues but also safely guides the therapeutic journey through the treacherous obstacles, which threaten the journey and outcome. It is critical for the clinician to pay strict attention to this as he or she sojourns through the abyss.

Marano Geiser (1990) also emphasizes the joining in the journey. She highlights the imperative of guiding the patient through darkness not as a leader but as a partner. Furthermore, she resists the temptation of ultimately resting in such a state but instead holds the therapist accountable toward "transformation into light" (p. 111). She also addresses the realm of shamanism and countertransference. Aptly, she clarifies the lack of boundaries that some shaman's experience when healing a patient. For some, the work literally requires "sucking out" the patient's illness and therefore internalizing the illness. This merging and mirroring of the patient's issues often leads to countertransference and in Marano Geiser's words, "does not allow for simple voyeurism" (p. 113). However, this reflection allows both the patient and the therapist to actualize the "many facetted experiences we live and the symbols we collectively share" (p. 113).

Ramseyer (1990) warns the art therapist not to be too quick to "clean up the client's life, organize the pain, or move the client through darkness too fast" (p. 116). She stresses the necessity in allowing client's not only ample time to wallow in this state but also warns the therapist of the need to pay attention to sorrow, frustration, and personal battles. I also have underscored this necessity when supervising my student interns. For it is so much easier to avoid the pain, loss, and need for mourning and instead move a patient all too quickly toward the light. If one avoids resonating with such suffering and protesting its entrance into treatment, then this anguish only raises its ugly head again and again until it thoroughly razes the patient's spirit and soul.

McNiff (1992) also emphasizes the danger in resisting the darkness. He, too, highlights the need to enfold this position as a means toward the end, that end being transformation and health. Furthermore, McNiff vehemently protests the pathology of the "therapeutic system" and instead urges "staff to openly accept the pathology of their interactions with one another" allowing for transformation. He states "pathology is not limited to patients" but is in fact in all of us and a "fundamental element of the soul" (p. 25). Therefore, McNiff, perhaps unknowingly, accentuates the inherent contradiction in visualizing a normal population.

Since he contends that pathology exists in all of us, and if one accepts that principle, then the concept of normalcy has in fact no place in our discussion. Still, researchers base their work on such norms and in the interest of science we need to acknowledge a "normal" population, at the very least, as well functioning. Still, within that context, we need to remove our blinders and anticipate the limitations attached to this position.

Like Ashbrook (1971), McNiff (1992) also notes the importance behind community. Eloquently, McNiff connects a patient's problems to a greater whole and states that the best medicine that he can suggest is to offer a patient a sense of purpose. In doing so, he proposes that the patient's suffering may indeed "contribute to the vitality of the community" and per force provide a process that is "reciprocal" (p. 25). Undeniably, these are medicinal words. By simply stating this profundity, McNiff lays the foundation for normalcy (e.g., well functioning) and prepares the canvas for layers of self-esteem, ego maturation, a sense of purpose, and above all, connectedness to a greater whole. Without this, there is little hope for contribution, aspiration, or a will to live. Humankind needs to have hope and purpose. Medicinal work *must* begin to orbit the heartbeat of community and its perpetual struggle for recognition and position. Failing to do so ignores the spirit, soul, and psyche of every human being. We must not fail this task, this calling. For whether or not the reader believes in God, a Higher Spirit, or embraces an agnostic or atheist position, this *is* our ilk, our therapeutic destiny. Aborting such a mission is surely to result in therapeutic failure and continued dis-ease.

Because the artist is often captivated by such social obligation, it seemed again a relatively obvious population to examine. For an artist's work always embodies communication and often engenders issues of social mores. Again, I pondered the possibilities and similarities of verbal and art responses, despite religious affiliation or creed. I attempted to test adults of varying beliefs and or non-beliefs in order to widen the spectrum. A former Jew, now atheist; a former Protestant, now Buddhist; a former Catholic, now agnostic; and a Latter Day Saint Mormon were among some of the subjects whom I tested and will present herein. Although there were varying responses from these four individuals, the art directive was an arduous task for most. Again, like other art therapy instruments, artistic prowess was not necessarily an advantage and for some it was a distinct disadvantage since there was an additional, self-imposed pressure to create something of artistic merit.

For a few, the interview provided reflection, which long past had been denied or repressed. For others, this seed translated into further questioning of the unknown and contemplation of the future. And for me, it offered a secondary gain, a chance to again connect with others and discuss this topic relegated to the sacred corridors of inquiry and thought. I relished these interviews. They offered not only insight into others but a place to leave behind all that is mundane and material in exchange for uniting on hallowed ground. Still, often as the administrant, I often felt rather voyeuristic and secretly harbored a desire to share my own stories and beliefs. I imagine that when conducting this interview, others will also fall prey to such temptations.

Yet, I urge the reader to abandon such thoughts since it would not only bias the results but perhaps be leading as well. Instead, when working with patients, one can later utilize this countertransferential press to share what would be salubrious to the health and transformation of the patient's life experiences.

## INTERVIEW WITH ROBERT, ATHEIST

At the time of testing, Robert, married with three children, was a 41-year-old art professor who had been raised Jewish and considered himself "ethnically Jewish" but currently determined himself an atheist. Because his twin brother actively participated in Yiddish jazz and was one of the leading authorities on Yiddish music and culture, Robert felt inevitably surrounded by this ethnicity. Yet, he avoided the traditional rituals such as attending synagogue, celebrating the Sabbath, and attending family Seders during the season of Passover. And although Robert was quick to state that he had a special interest in the Warsaw ghetto uprising and Nazi rallies, he clarified that he was able to separate this from everyday practice and belief in religion. He stated that both he and his twin brother struggled with religion while growing up and merely "went along" with their parents' expectations.

Naturally, this led to my asking if there was anything specifically that caused him to no longer believe in God. He responded, "I remember when I was a little kid, teachers would tell you to pray at night and do things like that and think of people. One experience I do remember was in first or second grade. One kid's house was on fire and his sister was in the hospital as a result of the fire. The teacher told us all to pray that she would get better and the next day she died. That kind of experience, you know, it's real easy to put two and two together and think, "Well, that didn't work." Of course, *When Bad Things Happen to Good People* and all that. . . . I hate self-help books, feel good books of any kind. I don't want any help, especially from myself . . . just little things would happen that you could tell there was absolutely no order to it at all, just a bunch of randomness that was flowing according to just contingency, basically. Not any higher power."

It seemed clear to me that Robert harbored great bitterness, although I couldn't extract specifically the cause of this angst and duress. So I asked him what his theories were of the universe and how it was created. His response was quite humbling.

Robert stated, "I think every person who thinks deeply enough about origins of things gets to a certain stopping point and that stopping point comes when you get to whether you believe in God or you believe in the Big Bang or primordial soup. There is always the ultimate question of how did God get there? How did the primordial soup get there? What was the Big Bang, how was it made, and how did it get there?

So I think all science and all religions stops at the same point and that point is completely unknowable, unimaginable, and ungraspable. And, the difference between people and me that have religion is that I admit that I haven't got a clue and other people think that for some reason, they have. That's all. It's a complete mystery to me, but I admit it."

Later on, during the discussion, Robert alluded to a fascination with the mystical and spiritual in art and literature. He clarified by expounding on his interest in ceremonial rituals, monuments, and the "questions that people formulate about why on earth they were put here." But, his attraction was purely observational and non-participatory.

As well, he professed that his own artwork was highly influenced by this quest. When I raised the question from what or whom Robert derived strength and meaning in his life, he responded that he received this by "accepting reality." He went on to explain: "From not relying on what I see as the crutch of belief and faith and instead facing the idea that it's all randomness and contingency, you can have an effect on it. . . . I accept that I try to do what I can in my world to make my life rich because I do believe in human relationships and I sort of believe in the here and now and I believe in the future and I believe in the past. I just don't believe there is anything or any force governing it. . . . I guess what I'm trying to say is that very lack of faith is what makes me strong. . . . I would hope that I would be able to rely on some inner strength."

Furthermore, Robert did not believe he had ever had a feeling of forgiveness. In fact, he felt that he would die feeling badly about certain things. This again gave me pause to contemplate what steered Robert toward self-preservation and relying only on himself. Not knowing him intimately, I could only wonder. Nevertheless, his artwork was intriguing. Since he did not believe in God, naturally the directive was to draw, paint, or sculpt what it was that he believed in and gave him strength and meaning in his life. I thought that he would create a self-portrait.

Like others faced with this task, he complained about how difficult it was to conceptualize the directive. Surprisingly enough, Robert created the world, Figure 5-1. He explained, "The concept is just the world as it is . . . not any heavens or anything, but just life on this planet (with) all its geographical reality and all its horrors and its beauty. . . . I've always liked land forms. They also change and are somewhat random and governed by the contingencies of nature. . . . It's hard to come up with a symbol of nothingness as far as faith goes. Another approach would have been to draw my wife or kids and my

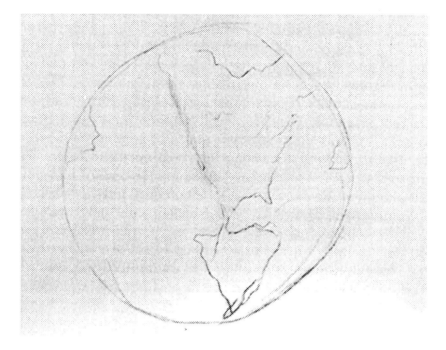

Figure 5-1. Robert's world.

mother and father and just the human personal relationships that are so vital to the world."

For the opposite, Robert drew Figure 5-2, describing it as "the standard sort of Michaelangelo God's figure." He elaborated by describing that for him the opposite was basically "all representations of the patriarch, Gods, old men with flowing beards, Santa Claus, et cetera. I could draw any number of representations (Christ on the Cross, Buddha, Zeus), just anything that people have invested their beliefs and represented in visual forms over the centuries. That would be the opposite." So for Robert, the concept of the graven image, of God, was the opposite of what he could believe in.

So in all this, how would Fowler view Robert's verbal associations to the interview and work produced? In discussing faith, Fowler purports that it is a "person's or group's way of moving into the force field of life . . . faith is a person's way of seeing him or herself in relation to others against a background of shared meaning and purpose" (1981, p. 4). While Robert denies having a faith or belief system, Fowler would argue this as a moot point. He states, "Whether we become nonbelievers, agnostics, or atheists, we are concerned with how to put our lives together and what will make life worth living. Moreover, we look for something to love that loves us, something to value that

Figure 5-2. Robert's patriarch.

gives us value, something to honor and respect that has the power to sustain our being" (1981, p. 5).

And so left with the task of assigning Robert a spiritual dimension as suggested by Fowler's stages of faith, one could conclude the following: Originally, Robert embraced Stage 1, Intuitive, Projective Faith, based on his undifferentiated love and trust for his parental figures. Within time, as he transgressed towards Stage 3, the Synthetic-Conventional stage of faith, he began to question the doctrines of his religious upbringing. As a result, he rejected Judaism and within time became a nonbeliever in God, resting comfortably within atheism. As Fowler purported, "interpersonal betrayals can give rise . . . to nihilistic despair about a personal principle of ultimate being" (1981, p. 173). Personal relationships are the driving power behind value and power.

So does this mean that Robert's spiritual development arrested? Certainly his level of artistic development goes way beyond the stages as outlined by Lowenfeld and Brittain (1975). Hence, one could profess that he had traversed into a stage that Lowenfeld and Brittain have not considered, something, which I have termed an Artistic Stage of Development. Yet, does this correlate with Fowler's stages of faith? Does it have to? If an Artistic Stage of Development were based on the concept of formed art expression as outlined by Kramer (1975), then that stage would represent the quintessential developmental stage of art. If that were to equivocate with Fowler's Stages of Faith (1981), then it would only be comparable to Stage 6, Universaling Faith. But considering the components of Stage 6, it would be unfair to place Robert in this category.

Unlike cognitive, emotional or physical development, can one's spiritual dimension be altered and *not* stunt humankind's potential for ego maturation and gratification? I'm not sure that I have the answers for that or more importantly, that I am able to judge such a question. Perhaps that mysterious query will remain unsolved. The closest rejoinder would be that this information would *only* have import and bearing *if* Robert's spiritual dimension suddenly caused undue duress. Robert's verbal responses and art results clearly reflect both his spiritual level of development and his spiritual dimension. This resulting information offers a wider spectrum for potential, operational standing, and specifically contributes to an overall understanding of his personality and mode of functioning. So in reviewing the Stages of Faith (according to Fowler, 1981) versus the Developmental Stages of Art (as outlined by Lowenfeld and Brittain, 1975), one can hypothesize that in some instance there might be overlap, but if there is not, it does not necessarily mean that the emotional arrestment will be equivocal in both comparisons. What it absolutely offers is multifaceted information about a human being regarding his or her systems of belief, faith, and functioning within the world. And as the reader will witness in subsequent chapters (such as Chapter 7), possessing this information in a clinical venue can make all the difference between success and failure in treatment.

## INTERVIEW WITH CAITLIN, AGNOSTIC

Caitlin, married with three children, was 36 years old at the time of the interview. In college, she had trained to be an artist but currently was a homemaker for her three young boys. When I asked Caitlin when she first became agnostic, she stated that the death of her first husband (approximately 13 years prior) had influenced this decision. Yet, she admitted that she had doubts in high school and college and as young as age eight. She stated, "I guess I just was starting to think when I was a really young kid. I remember hearing my father say, 'And now they are letting Protestants into Heaven!' I remember thinking, "That means all these people aren't going to Heaven. You think that just these people are going to go on?" And I think he was kind of, you know . . . it was shaky for him, too."

Caitlin also spoke of truly becoming agnostic when her first husband developed a brain tumor and died shortly after his treatment began. She spoke of the Catholic traditions being "beautiful," yet she did not believe in "one religion." Instead, she sustained that the purpose of being on earth was to "include everybody." In expounding about this agnostic conversion, she explained, "He really needed those priests, when he went into the hospital. We didn't know exactly what was wrong, but he was sick, and I made a point of telling the doctors, "This is the church he belongs to and he really does want priests to come visit."

"The first time one came, he didn't come past the doorway, and maybe he assumed that he was alone and must be contagious. It was the most bizarre thing. I wasn't there, but when I came in and he said, "Yeah, he came. But, he wouldn't go past the door," I knew that it really hurt him, and I was really amazed. I guess I was amazed and really disappointed somebody I always looked to for some compassion and comfort couldn't get past the doorway in his room."

Caitlin felt quite alienated at this time. Yet she relayed a story of the priest who had married them and how her husband, then bald and scarred from surgical intervention and treatment, sheepishly admitted how "ugly" he was. The priest sincerely responded, "You look like Jesus Christ to me." That was what Caitlin "had been looking for." In all this, she had not completely lost her faith. She explained, "It's interesting. I was thinking being there with him when he died is probably the reason I didn't lose my faith completely because something amazing happened! You know, I mean that maybe, I really do think there's something there, there's something beyond. And that is probably the reason I didn't just give up completely; I just stopped putting it all in one basket."

When I asked her if she could share what led to this decision, I simultaneously apologized for asking such personal questions. Tears came to her eyes as she recounted the event and she bravely confirmed, "Oh no, I don't mind because I think it's absolutely amazing. I mean, I think that it's too bad we don't talk about, can't share this part of our lives with the whole world." She then apologized for being so "disconnected." I assured her that this was in fact "very connected" and urged her to go on.

"Well, when he died, just a couple of minutes before, we knew that it was coming. He looked at me and his eyes were *so* blue. His eyes had been so dulled by, I don't know, by being very, very sick, but then they were suddenly so blue. It was just completely amazing and I just cried out, "What's happening to you? What's happening?" I was stunned and he cried, I mean a tear came out of his eye. I know everything I had not been able to tap into kept coming out.

"Luckily this nurse who was a friend of ours grabbed me, basically holding me together from behind and kept saying, 'Tell him that you love him.' And, then I guess I said something like 'You're reaching across, you're almost there.' I don't remember saying it. But, I remember hearing it."

I asked her if she felt she was actually seeing him "cross over." And she responded, "That's what it felt like to me. It was all in the way he looked at me and it was so true. It gives me the shivers. . . . He just basically pulled away. His mother was on the other side, which was kind of interesting to me; that we were on opposite sides of him and he just pulled his shoulders away, as if he were pulling away from here."

When I inquired as to what kind of relationship she had with God, she responded, "I don't have this specific thing or idea, it's just that I still feel something. And I feel like there's something there; I just don't know how to communicate. I don't know how to make the communication that used to be directed through prayer. But I guess I have this belief and reverence for this thing, for lack of a better word, that I think is out there and is part of what people really are."

When asked what gave her strength and meaning in her life she answered, "Yeah, I guess it really is when I think of my father and especially Mike (first husband). I don't know how to express it. To see that you don't stop loving and that this relationship stays there even though you're separated is so amazing. I think probably it's the people in my life that have done that and definitely my parents and my family and my first relationship with Mike. But also the experience that I learned; he taught me a lot in going through this with him, and my second husband, Randy, I mean he's an unusual character for a person whose emotions just don't show. And, it's so deep inside of him. To see that you don't stop loving and that this relationship stays there even though you're separated is so amazing that I don't know, I guess the bottom line is what people give you along the way. That's what does it."

*What people give you along the way.* An intriguing way of wrapping up what makes us what we are. And interestingly enough, this brings me back to community and its inherent importance in self-sustaining a sense of purpose, the will to go on. For some, relying on God and pinning one's faith in this vehicle is the way to extract strength and meaning in one's life. And, for others, a sense of community and what one has received from others is the vantage point.

When I asked Caitlin whether or not she had ever felt a sense of forgiveness, she spoke about her decision to leave the Catholic Church as an "acknowledgement, a sort of passage, something that (she) needed to do."

Caitlin chose not to create an opposite since she had difficulty contending with such a configuration and instead only responded to the first directive. Figure 5-3 is Caitlin's rendition of what God means to her. Although she felt

Figure 5-3. Caitlin's light.

quite awkward while working on it, she seemed at great peace, humming as she worked. She knew exactly what she wanted to make but expressed not only how difficult it was to create but, moreover, how discomforting it was "to be watched." Again, I felt the need to apologize for my voyeurism.

She explained how she viewed God: "I always see it as a black sky with light. And that's always there. When I was younger, I would spend time either praying or thinking and it was usually at night. I guess I always had this picture of there being light. That's the best way I can describe it. That's the way I always thought of God, I guess, is light."

## THE LIGHT

Others, too, have made this connection of God as light. It came up repeatedly in the artwork and verbal associates of the clergy whom I tested. And, scores of books, including both the Old and New Testaments, have also claimed that God has appeared in the form of light. Furthermore, others in discussing near-death experiences (NDE's) have also described a passage into light or a tunnel of light.

One of the best selling books of our time, *Embraced by the Light,* written by Eadie (1992), claimed that she did in fact die (and her medical doctor attested and confirmed this fact) only to return to this earth and continue her mission. When her mission on earth is finished, and only then, would she return to this other dimension that renounces boundaries and time, as we know it in our earthly state. This book is an extraordinary tale and a compelling read.

Some have called her story "ancient" and a tale that has in fact been passed down for generations but only now has been published. Several of the claims she makes may appear radical, albeit impossible to many. For example, when she was in the presence of the Lord, she "saw that all things were created by a spiritual power. Each element, each particle of creation, has intelligence in it, which intelligence is filled with spirit and life, and thus the capacity for experiencing joy" (1992, p. 57).

Moreover, she professed an understanding that "life is lived most fully in the imagination—that, ironically, *imagination* is the key to reality. This is something I never would have supposed. We are sent here to live fully, to live it *abundantly,* to find joy in our own creations, whether they are new thoughts or *things* or emotions or experiences" (1992, p. 59).

Two things, which are mentioned in the aforementioned paragraph had specific bearing on my work. The first was that "*imagination* is the key to reality." As an artist, plagued by my collective demons, I have always wondered why in fact I was bestowed with not only the gift of an untamed, unrestrained imagination but also the additional burden and simultaneous pleasure of visually creating that cogitation, which leads me to Eadie's second point: We are sent here and have a definitive purpose in our earthly existence.

Eadie (1992) described a state of watching the earth's creation and watching "spirit brothers and sisters (enter) physical bodies for their turns upon the earth, each experiencing the pains and joy that would help them progress" (1992, p. 52). Furthermore she stated, "I knew that only those who needed that experience were placed there. I saw the angels rejoicing for those who endured their trials and succeeded and grieving for those who failed. I saw that some failed for their own weaknesses, and some failed because of the weaknesses of others. . . . We are where we need to be. . . . I saw that we all volunteered for our positions and stations in the world and that each of us is receiving more help than we know. . . . I saw the unconditional love of God. . . . I would give all in my power, all that I ever was, to be filled with that love again—to be embraced in the arms of his eternal light" (1992, p. 52–53). Of course, someday when she dies and does not come back, perhaps she will experience this unconditional love again. And, in fact, if her message bears truth, that we "volunteered for our positions" and lots in life, perhaps hers was to bring this truth to humankind.

So, in essence, this "primordial soup" does contain a divine scheme of things and more importantly perhaps our individual and collective lives really do have meaning and are not a "contingent randomness," as suggested by Robert. And if Eadie is correct in her assumption that intelligent spirit permeates every element of creation, then in fact, whether a person is murderous or saintly, God is by definition in all of us. And if we can believe that, then in fact, wouldn't that need for community be the same thing as the need for God?

The devil's advocate might contend here, "What about the hermit, the monk, the recluse?" Eadie's answer might be that the spirit does in fact breathe "an intelligence," a pulse if you will, in all things. Therefore, one is never truly alone since (according to Eadie (1992), God is a part of us all. Whether one's intention is good or evil, as delineated by Eadie (1992), it is all part of a greater plan, an outline defined by God. And, this, of course, brings back one thing that Fowler (1981) meant to impress so deeply onto his readers: the importance of faith. Alas, where there is hope, there is life—that is as we know it as earthly human beings.

So what about dear Caitlin? Where does her artwork place her in the index of spiritual dimension? Like Robert, is she, too, stuck in Stage 3, the Synthetic-Conventional stage? Clearly, by her agnostic position, she belonged more in the realm of those who walk the corridors of Stage 4, the Individuative-Reflective Stage. People who roam these hallways question their responsibilities for their own commitment, lifestyle, belief, and attitudes. Unavoidable tensions surface in this stage. Struggle with the absolute is at a premium at this point and instead the commitment is to the relative, the known. According to Fowler (1981), Stage 4 generally occurs between the mid 30s and early 40s.

Thus, developmentally, Caitlin was clearly at the appropriate age of onset. Moreover, she experienced many of the nodal events that often catapult people from Stage 3 to Stage 4 (e.g., changes in primary relationships, death, growing up, leaving home) (Fowler, 1981, p. 181).

Nevertheless, age need not be a predictor of spiritual maturation. However, life experience may certainly contribute to the index of spiritual development. Yet, neither age nor life experience can be the determining factor since one need only look to history as a disputing agent. Transformation seems to defy both definition and description. Like music, its want, while often inspiring, seems to resist categorization and knows no boundaries.

## INTERVIEW WITH KAREN, BUDDHIST

At interview, Karen was 44 years old, currently employed as a secretary, and a practicing artist and Zen Buddhist. Although she grew up as a nonpracticing Protestant and had a deep belief in God, by her adolescence, she no longer adhered to those beliefs. At that point, she stopped believing in God. As an adult, she described herself as agnostic. But soon, her work as an artist became the catalyst behind her interest in Buddhism. Reading about the field had led Karen toward this practice as opposed to a specific quest or search for meaning. Although it is not required to live at the Zen Center, Karen chose to do so for approximately one and a half years. She joined the community, called a Songa, and became an integral part of the staff.

When I inquired what it meant to actually be on staff, Karen replied that everyone in the Songa was assigned certain tasks. At one point, hers was cooking. But she explained that being on staff did not require instruction but to sit and meditate intensively for many hours a day. Job-related duties are structured around the sitting since the practice of Zen Buddhism requires meditation.

Although Karen no longer lives at the Zen Center, her commitment involves "sitting" both morning and night. She explained, "I get up at 4 o'clock in the morning, leave about 4:30. There is a formal sitting for a little more than an hour, but I usually leave earlier than that. Then there are a few hours in the evening from 7 to 9 when we sit. I do that as well."

Likewise, while discussing her relationship with both the Songa and the Abbot (Zen Master), Karen explained that the Songa is similar to a church community in that the group participates in activities together. However, there is the opportunity to meet with the Abbot on a one-to-one basis, called a deaccession. This meeting is confidential. The process requires turning inward and finding one's "root source," akin to a "nature of inquiry." Yet, she explained, "There is no God in Buddhism. There is no external source to yourself that one would identify as God. . . . Beyond subatomic particles, what do you have?"

In discussing her religious practices, Karen referred to a practice of sitting cross-legged, with back erect, and eyes slightly lowered, focusing on whatever the Abbot assigns as a point of meditation. As well, incense is lit and there is a Buddha sculpture on an altar. However, these acts are not to be confused with idolatry. Instead, they are meant to merely represent Buddha nature, a form of Zen inquiry. For some these devotional rituals assist the meditation process, but for Karen, it was not an essential part of Buddhism. She elucidated, "If you want to talk about a belief system, it's the belief that everything is not dual, there is a total unity to everything. Again, you could compare this to quantum physics."

Still somewhat confused, I inquired whether or not this "unity" was ever involved in her problems. She replied, "Again, an interesting question because the nature of inquiry is to let go of all thoughts and attachments and to try and turn the mind back to the source. . . . As the mind quiets, it gets to a place where there is no thought. . . . My way of understanding the Buddhist practices is that there is no blame attached to anything. Phenomena arise out of the mind but there is no judgment attached to that. There really is no bad or good. Those are just simply concepts and name tags we attach to phenomena. There's no judgment attached to that."

Furthermore she clarified that the concept of forgiveness might be a sense of joy and peace extracted from the meditating, a quality of the mind that she would describe as peace rather than forgiveness.

Naturally, when giving Karen the first directive, I asked her to draw, paint, or sculpt what Buddhism meant to her. Choosing black, tempera paint, she very quickly delineated Figure 5-4, a simple representation of a flower. She informed me that Zen is intrinsically tied into art making and that since her involvement in Buddhism, she has practiced enaugraphy. When I asked her if she could explain her art response, she said, "For me, it's life, it manifests itself in everything. It could have been any object. The flower has an association with Buddhism because the Buddha at one point held up a flower in front of an assembly. One of his monks smiled and received an understanding from it, from what he was demonstrating. It's that association. So is life. Every moment in everything."

Karen said that she had witnessed that state which she was describing and articulated that she felt "joyful" about the work, yet unable to verbally articulate what she meant by this. Furthermore, she could not create its opposite since she reiterated that would be dualistic, a concept in which she didn't believe.

She simplified, "There is no subject and no object. No identification at all, so your question implies judgment. In order for there to be something opposite to that, there has to be a subject. If there are two things there is a dualism there. . . . There is just human nature. You are whole and complete as you are. The synopsis of Buddhism lies in four norms of truth: Life is suffering is the first normal truth. You come to have that. In my own experience, you have an understanding of that and there is a cause of suffering, which is desire or attachment. . . . Suffering is caused by the way the mind sees and attaches to things and you act out of that. These are kind of habitual responses. And then the second normal truth is that there is a way out. The third normal truth is actually suffering; there is a way for suffering to cease, which is through realization of your true nature. The fourth normal truth is that there is a way to achieve that realization. Through Zen Buddhism, we approach that through meditation and our particular traditions. Its liberation is the basis of unity. The eye with which you see God is the eye which sees you. That's a pretty good way of expressing what Zen Buddhism is all about."

Well, that gave me pause! "The eye with which you see God is the eye which sees you." Again, Eadie's treatise (1992) came to mind as well as the

Figure 5-4. Karen's flower.

response of Rabbi Mark to the art-making process. Silently I mused, aren't we all talking about the same thing? This "inquiry," as Karen put it, seemed to be at the root of not only all suffering but also the pathway to true transformation and realization.

Clearly, Karen's thinking placed her at Stage 6, Universalizing Faith. "The self at Stage 6 engages in spending and being spent for the transformation of present reality in the direction of a transcendent actuality" (Fowler & Keen, 1978, p. 89). The bearers of Stage 6, whether they stand in Jewish, Christian, Islamic, or other traditions, manifest this leaning into the future for all being. What separates these persons from others is in Fowler's words, their ability to:

> kindle our imaginations . . . because in their generosity and their authority, in their freedom and their costly love, they embody the promise and lure of our shared futurity. . . . They actualize its promise, creating zones of liberation and sending shock waves to rattle the cages that we allow to constrict human futurity. Their trust in the power of that future and their trans-narcissistic love of human futurity account for their readiness to spend and be spent in making the Kingdom actual. (1981, p. 211)

### INTERVIEW WITH RENFRED, LATTER DAY SAINT MORMON

Upon interview, Renfred was an art history professor, aged 58, a fifth generation, Latter Day Saint Mormon, married, and the father of eight children. When I asked what his involvement was with his temple, he explained that he functioned as a bishop for his congregation: "We have no paid ministry, so it's all volunteer. So a bishop is called to oversee a congregation in a priest role function. And, he has to counsel people. I think most of the time when we are in a counseling situation, we . . . rely a lot on professionals."

Currently, if Renfred had problems, he would seek out another bishop in order to air his concerns. When asked about specific rituals or practices that he found meaningful, he mentioned that he fasted: "It's partly a social thing that we abstain from eating two meals; it's usually the supper meal on Saturday and the breakfast meal on Sunday. And then the equivalent of money that we would have spent on those meals goes to the poor. And it's called the Fast Offering. Individuals in the congregation or individuals at large, they don't have to be members of the church to receive any, get that money to help pay their rent or to keep their lights or electricity on. On most Sundays, we ask different members of the congregation to talk on prepared subjects. On Fast Sunday, nobody is asked ahead of time to speak and the meeting is turned over to the congregation and if people feel like it, they get up and express their gratitude for their friendships or their family or just express themselves right from the heart and . . . sometimes it's rather bizarre, but most of the time it's much more immediate and real. So I think that's a special thing."

When I asked what his relationship was like with God, he responded, "As a family, we say prayers both in the morning and in the evening. Then we fast. We try to read the scriptures once a day–generally for five or ten minutes. Often, that's left to private time, however you want to do that. I can only speak for myself. I don't know how other people's relationships are or how real that is to them. In a lot of ways, Delores, my wife, is a big part of my life, the person I consult the most about my feelings. And what am I doing, and where am I going, and how am I doing. "

When I asked Renfred what gave him special strength and meaning in his life, he replied, "I think the family, both immediate and extended, the churches concept of a life after death . . . experiences that are hard." Moreover, when I questioned if God was ever involved in his problems, Renfred responded, "Well, He's involved in the sense that He sometimes removes stumbling blocks or makes our pathway easier so we don't stub our toe too often. I think that He's caring and able to lend that kind of emotional support.

"We believe in free agency. We are an agent to act for ourselves. If He came in and manipulated things for us, then He's in control and not us. So, in that sense, I don't think He's involved in our problems that He's either made them or can remove them. But problems are one of the reasons that we are here. . . . We feel that the main reason that we are here is to serve others and to develop "pure love" if we are going to be worthy.

"Mormonism is a little bit unique and strange in that we believe we existed in a pre-existent state. We believe that in the pre-existing state, we were literally spirits . . . and that we wanted to become like Him and in order to do that we have to pass through a mortal existence and develop the way He became, and we believe that fathers and sons can become like the Heavenly Father and Heavenly Mother and that we have the potential to become godly."

(I bristled at this since while the comparison that *"fathers and sons"* could become "like" divine beings (including the "Heavenly Mother"), there was no mention as to whether or not *women* could achieve this same ascension within this religion.)

It reminded me of my desire to follow in my great, great grandfather's footsteps, the great Rabbi Bachrach, the former Chief Rabbi of New England. Suddenly, I was swept back to my age six, listening to the Cantor in temple. Already fluent in reading Hebrew, I turned to my father and announced that I wanted to be a Rabbi when I grew up. His response, "You can't. You're a girl," horrified me. I sat sullenly for the rest of the Friday night service and began to think of my options as a "girl." Is it no wonder that I am still searching for that piece of me, lost in the dreams of oppression as a child?)

Recently, I shared this story for the first time with another art therapist who grew up Jewish yet now practices in a Yoga tradition. When he confessed that he, too, once shared the same aspiration, it really made me wonder about what propels us to search for a spiritual existence. Naturally, I did not share this with Renfred, but I offer this countertransferential response to the reader as a warning: for this may bring up many unresolved issues from your own familial and spiritual wanderings.

Regarding a sense of forgiveness, Renfred expounded on his viewpoint: "I think it's different in a sense that you don't get forgiveness just by saying, 'Heavenly Father, last night I went out and slept with three women and I'm sorry. Forgive me,' and the slate's wiped clean. Forgiveness is something that only occurs when a heart-felt change takes place. Then, once that has been demonstrated, the incident or past sin or whatever it is becomes erased from memory."

Not knowing much about the Book of Mormon, I asked how it differed from other scriptures. Renfred maintained that they [other scriptures] were additional and contained certain truths. He also explained that Mormons didn't believe in infant baptism. In the Book of Mormon, in order to be baptized, one had to reach the "age of accountability." One had to know right from wrong.

He elaborated, "We believe when Jesus was on the Earth and established His church, that there was no infant baptism. Through the course of assimilation of the Roman Empire and Greek philosophy and so forth, many of the correct things were lost and people strayed. But that's just one case—the baptism—the knowledge of a pre-existence—the belief in the afterlife. For instance, we don't believe in eternal Hell. We don't believe that that's the end of it. When you die, you still have the opportunity in your state of waiting, when your body is separated from your spirit, you still can be taught. You can still accept. That's why we have temples, for instance, to do baptisms for the dead. We do the work, because baptism being an earthly ordinance has to be done for them, and they have the opportunity to accept it or reject it. If one wishes to be baptized for a dead person, then someone can go in as a proxy. So the first time I go through the temple is for myself. Any time I go subsequently thereafter, I take the name of the deceased person. I function as a proxy for that person. And I go through the anointments and the washings and whatever with the idea that it's done, and that deceased person has the right to accept it or reject it."

When I asked Renfred to draw, paint or sculpt what it was that God meant to him, he stated, "What He means to me? That is tough. I don't know how to draw intelligence or how to draw a life. Our world is not the only world that God has created. He has created worlds without number. But, I feel that they would be like us. I can't do it with markers, because pure intelligence, enlightened truth, far exceeds our ability."

I next inquired as to how he felt about what he had created (Figure 5-5). He stated that it was "inadequate." That this was "not something we can do in this life. We have eternities to figure out God." As well, Renfred stated that he had never witnessed God as he had drawn him.

I then asked him to specify how he felt about his work. He commented, "I'm sure everybody feels this way, but the idea that my ways are not your ways, and my thoughts are not your thoughts, and so forth. That we, as mortals, differ so much where we are at this point from where He is that you can't with drawings or anything show that gap . . . that difference."

Next, I asked him if he believed in an opposite force to God and if he did, if he could create that. He responded, "Mormons believe, literally, that just as Jesus was the only begotten son in this life, that in the preexistence there was another son, Lucifer, who was the son of light, a son of the morning, who is also very intelligent and who rebelled against God and was cast out with his followers. And a third of the hosts of heaven were cast out. And their role is to prevent us from fulfilling this plan, because they rebelled against the plan.

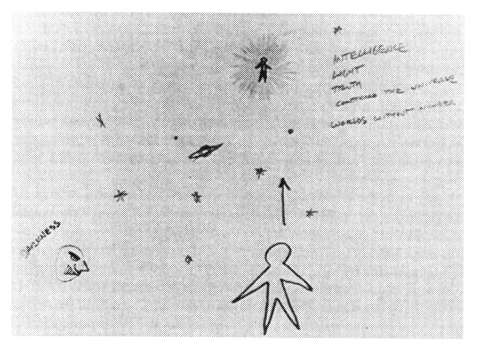

Figure 5-5. Renfred's response.

I guess what I would do is . . . darkness, but still with a lot of intelligence and powers because He [Lucifer] has such intelligence that he can deceive. He has the ability to be very sophisticated. He can make good seem bad and bad seem good. If I could get cartoon-like, he'd be a sly guy. He would be an individual just like all of us. . . . But he has an inordinate amount of greed, and He wanted to usurp God's power. So his role is to frustrate. He is a very sophisticated, sly kind of person who masks the real message, like a car salesman."

When asked if he had ever witnessed Lucifer or that darkness he was expounding on, Renfred replied, "I've experienced what I would say mental states in which I feel I was moving towards this. Or when I'm in a state where I feel like I'm not being true to myself that I have not been doing always the things that I know to be right, then I feel this kind of darkness. I feel this kind of depression. I do believe that it is possible to give yourself over to those influences to a point where those influences take control. And at some point then, you virtually are a prisoner either through addiction of some kind or another."

Renfred's comparison of darkness and depression was not a foreign concept. I had witnessed this controlling power, incapacitating many of my patients and leaving them emasculated, impotent in the fight for health. Moreover, his insight of falling "prisoner" to such workings also concurred with many of my patients' struggles. This suggested "addiction" was verily an apt descriptor for this rein of melancholy. Truly, it is easier to remain "sick" than to move towards wellness and recovery. For the latter is an unknown province. And the unfamiliar territory of wellness, despite its salubrious nature, is far more threatening than accepting the predetermined, well-known terrain of despair.

In examining Renfred's response and accompanying artwork (Figure 5-5), similar notions arise. Again, the concept of light and intelligence gets factored in to both the discussion and actual work. Moreover, Renfred's concept of man transcending towards God and having the ability to become "godly" concurs with Eadie's (1992) position of our purpose and mission in life. And like others who were tested before him, the idea of light became a repeated schema (see results from the clergy, Chapter 4, and Caitlin, this chapter).

So what does this mean? Does it suggest anything more than some kind of collective unconscious seeding itself in the human mind? And because Renfred's artistic style is clearly primitive as opposed to technically realistic, does it subsume that his artwork is developmentally lower than others tested before him? Or should one analyze only the verbal associates to the artwork and responses to the interview in order to obtain a person's spiritual dimension as well as his stage of faith?

Clearly, Renfred's verbal responses to the queries suggest that he vacillates somewhere between Stage 4, Individuative-Reflective Faith, and Stage 5, Conjunctive Faith. However, based on the Mormon tradition of a "proxy baptism" for those not converted to this religion, Renfred clearly waffles more towards a Stage 4 existence. "Its dangers inherent in its strengths: an excessive confidence in the conscious mind and in critical thought and a kind of second narcissism in which the now clearly bounded, reflective self overassimilates "reality" and the perspectives of others into its own world view" (Fowler, 1981, pp. 182–183).

And does the developmental level of artwork offer any clue to nodal issues or spiritual arrestment? Of that, I am unsure. Clearly, the responses both verbally and artistically offer insight into a person's belief system and offer the clinician an additional path for operation and understanding systems functioning. And perhaps that is truly all that matters.

As Natal (1994) recently stated regarding imagery:

> There's a distinction between description and interpretation. It's important for students to think about what they bring to looking at art. Understanding . . . imagery and how . . . (this) has influenced culture is more about investigation than about prescribed history. (p. 3)

Analyzing the data specifically as it applies to each individual is more in keeping with spiritual development than narrowing the study for the purpose of addressing commonalities between artistic stages of development and the stages of a person's faith. More importantly, the information extracted can contribute to a greater understanding of a person's background and the transitional conflicts handed down from generation to generation. And ruling out religiosity as a predictor of pathology is equally important to the task. Instead, one needs to "care for the soul" (as suggested by Moore, 1992) and its constant drive toward recognition and transcendence. By embracing these parameters, one can, in fact, begin to do that. Alas, no longer ignoring the person's spiritual dimension, a clinician can finally operate on the matters of the heart and care for the soul.

# Chapter 6

# SPIRITUAL ART THERAPY:
# A WORKING ALTERNATIVE FOR
# EMOTIONALLY DISTURBED
# CHILDREN AND YOUTH

> The picture of God we make for ourselves is
> parallel with our inner development.
>
> –Henricson-Cullberg, 1984

For over 25 years, I have specialized in working with emotionally disturbed children and youth both in residential treatment and through my private practice. Based on my experiences, it seems abundantly obvious that a person's own moral precepts are, by necessity, fashioned on the foundations of one's parental or environmental constitutions. Exactly when this principle comes into play is, in fact, debatable. The very young child of approximately three to five years of age is verily imprinted and indoctrinated by this circumstantial upbringing. Yet according to Lowenfeld and Brittain (1975), the age of reasoning doesn't begin until the maturational age of 12. However, I believe that one's moral reasoning, while influenced by parental and/or environmental factors, can commence as early as eight or nine years of age. It is around that age that a child actively socializes outside of the familial schema in an attempt to "fit in" and make sense of the world.

Piaget (1966) refers to this stage of development as concrete operational. Kohlberg (1969) would add that heteronomous morality and instrumental exchange are the hallmarks of this developmental period. And Fowler (1981) would categorize this stage as falling in that of Mythic-Literal Faith. But clearly, passage into this "stage of faith" development hinges on acceptance of one's surrounding tenets. Transition beyond this point occurs only through questioning.

Therefore, the spiritual development of a person clearly cannot be tested or predicted much before the age of eight. It is at this age that the clinician could utilize the BATA in the hope of measuring a person's *own* belief system. Nevertheless, in cases where younger children arrive into treatment as the identified patient (IP), one can look to the family system for answers. Oftentimes, the belief system of families can adversely affect the mental health and stability of a child in treatment, specifically if the family is tied to religious doctrines that are punitive in nature. In that case, it is often instrumental to work either from a family systems perspective and/or individual-oriented family therapy based on the psychodynamic model.

> Until recent times, the child was defined for parents in terms of possession. Parents had undisputed ownership of children and could deal with them as righteously as they wished. Disciplinary measures, if applied, were swift, sharp, and final. (Halpern & Kissel, 1976, p. 118)

Cogent sociopsychological assumptions are encompassed by family therapist Bell (1961, 1974). Therapeutic goals are family-centered even when the child was in individual treatment. This method attempts to bring about both attitudinal and behavioral changes in order to repair the disorder in intrafamilial communication and interaction. The two primary factors that influence these modes of treatment are to encourage verbal and affective expression while simultaneously fostering disciplined decision making in intrafamilial communication and interaction. While these may appear incongruent, according to Halpern and Kissel (1976), "it is the integration of divergent elements whereby families become more resilient and gain in strength" (p. 120). Moreover, if families understand their differences and simultaneous need for structural interdependence, respect for each other as individual human beings might have a greater chance for accord.

Furthermore, in such a climate, spirituality can also subsist. Without such atmosphere, spirituality has little to no chance for existence nor blossom. Encouraging this milieu is, by far, the most important element for inspiring the creative spirit to inhabit not only the identified patient but also the family system. Although seemingly simple, fostering the ground for spirituality is in itself paradoxically complex. Oftentimes, leading by example is the only penetrative method for operational functioning. However, when questioning the familial belief system, the clinician creates an atmospheric condition that *invites* discussion of the soul. Interviewing the family system members without this incorporation contributes to further dissonance and disarray. Therefore, the therapist *must* embrace the familial belief system, observe the offending pattern, and enter the family gestalt via improved interaction. However, this task is impossible to complete unless the practitioner truly understands the familial belief system and modus operandi for systems functioning.

The questions that precede the BATA offer a springboard for grasping
these family myths and expose clues for acumen and change. And in this, the
clinician must attend to this knowledge, co-create and reconstruct the system.
*Mindful* listening is the key to such success. Although this may seem terribly
obvious, it is the emphasis on "mindful" that needs to ensue. Co-creating such
interactive dynamics requires the therapist to be respectful of the familial
belief system, to infiltrate the operational patterns, and to change it from within. While this might sound theoretically correct but smack of functional
impossibility, I *assure* you it is not. It demands flexibility, creativity, and the-
atrical demonstration. But these describers are no more than garb that adorns
the uniform of the most effective therapists. Judith Rubin (1984) eloquently
wrote about this in her opus, *The Art of Art Therapy:* "*Flexibility* refers to the
ability to perceive the same thing in different ways, to shift gears from one
frame of reference to another, and to deal with unforeseen events with minimal frustration" (p. 18). Not an easy task. It is the "minimal frustration" that
hoodwinks most people because the "frustration" to which Dr. Rubin refers is
*not* just the patient's but also the therapist's.

Herein lies the rub. The alias of countertransference generally raises its
ugly countenance about here. But the loathsome nature of countertransference need not be fetid. Instead, as I have suggested in the past (Horovitz-
Darby, 1992), it can be a gift. But one needs to view it as such, otherwise
accepting the offensive belief system of others requires more than mere the-
atrics. And if the therapist does not rise to this occasion, then the remarks and
actions are viewed as saccharin and impure. In order to be believed and truly
alter the system, one needs to temporarily adopt this *Zeitwelt,* verily try it on,
wear it, and above all understand it. Otherwise, all meaning is lost both for
the interpreter (therapist) and for the patient. In doing so, one actually
**becomes** part of the family system. And as Halpern and Kissel point out, this
is the only way to change the system from within:

> Moreover, like the parents, the therapist affirms how he is on the side of the
> children, the only difference being in that he knows how to make parents more
> aware of their feelings and desires. He proceeds to point out to the children that
> the mother and the father want to deal with them differently for the happiness
> of all. . . . Finally, he invokes the paradoxic principle of family group therapy,
> namely of being the umpire who, during the sessions, enforces the rules he
> makes. . . . By taking an active role with regard to changing communicational
> patterns and by applying these skills to practical methods of interpersonal dis-
> course and environmental manipulation, the therapist introduces a sense of
> order and mastery into the proceedings. (1976, pp. 121–129)

Although this might seem inherently simple, the therapist must be short of
a magician in order to effectuate both transformation and transcendence. This
requires great skill, but above all, patience. For altering the family dynamics,

which have been persistently operational, is a formidable challenge. Shaking up the homogeneous components and exacting heterogeneous results are *always* resisted. The old maxim that "it is easier to remain sick than to get well" is never more accurately applicable than when working with resistant family systems. And in working with the families of children in residential treatment, I have found that it is *not* just the children who desire to remain "ill" and continue to be coddled by a milieu treatment approach, but more correctly, it is the *family system* that resists wellness and recovery and instead craves the addictive care taking. The reasons are as varied as the families whom I have treated. *What they share in common, however, is the secondary gain that they all seem to adduce from remaining ill.* And what the practitioner needs to learn is to *resist* the notion of becoming an unwilling member of the system that sets the stage for such *codependent posture.* In order to avoid such conduct, one needs to understand not only this inherent danger but also the distinguishing factors of working with children in residential treatment.

## ENVIRONMENTAL CONSIDERATIONS

**Troubled children.** According to Halpern and Kissel (1976), society has developed myriad ways to cope with this animal. Generations prior, meddlesome youngsters were sent to a variety of retreats in order to both relieve the taxed parents of their stressful situation and to distance the offending child for a respite and desired "cure." Oftentimes, this "mini-vacation" would take the shape of a summer vacation to a dear relative's or, if unavailable, sublimation was ordered in the form of apprenticeship. As society became more attuned to the parental need of bypassing the family tension, summer camps were developed for similar reasons. However way one can frame this, the bottom line was that separation was the intention for preserving and salvaging the family system even when developmental maturation and increased independence were the only aim. If nothing else, diffusion was a result. Alas, unfortunately for some children, the disunion did not lead to reparation but rather fostered emotional scars.

Then there were the truly homeless, the vagabonds and societal rejects that no one wanted. Fortunately for these children, society developed yet another manner for housing their troubled souls. Perhaps due to civilization's inherent maturation and conviction for preserving the human spirit, community centers, residential placements, foster care, adoptive agencies, independent living programs, and a medley of alternative domains sprung up. Yet people also viewed these solutions as mixed blessings. On the one hand, the public was relieved of this burden while on the other, "it clung to the belief that institutional care at best was static and more often than not led to deterioration" (Halpern & Kissel, 1976, p. 18). Others, too, maintained this position that nurturance by primary caretakers improved the chances of engendering well-adjusted, healthy individuals (see Bowlby, 1951; Spitz, 1965).

Since institutions were perceived as unnatural replacements for the primary caretaker, the thrust moved toward placement into foster families and adoption. Yet for those juveniles who flunked out of such holding tanks, the notion of residential placement became a viable (and hopefully), temporary solution. Oddly enough, the convalescent child more often than not survived in this environment, which substituted nutrients, affection, grooming, order, and regimen for inadequate, neglectful care. Other incorrigible offenders were sometimes placed in state schools in order to both protect society and the child from his or her own ills. Some of these youth were under court jurisdiction and frowned upon these arrangements, perceiving the installation as punitive and sullied. By the late 1960s, it became recognized that housing such individuals in large centralized care was deleterious (see Rabin, 1965; Edwards, 1968; LaVietes et al., 1960). Instead the direction moved toward decentralization: batches of residential cottages, group homes, and independent living situations, thus reducing the penal aspect of their injury (Halpern & Kissel, 1976). Moreover, the hallmark of such programs was the involvement of the family system and community at large.

## RESIDENTIAL TREATMENT: THE WARP AND THE WOOF

Nowadays, children are not simply whisked away, hidden from society, and never seen again. Instead, the aim is to incorporate these youngsters into both the fabric of society and bosom of the family. By design, these programs are created to produce significant change without disrupting the family life but rather incorporating its existence into the treatment mode. While this intention is an honorable one, the aforementioned design sometimes remains as imaginative as its construct, utterly unachievable.

At one such particular agency where I worked, this structure girdled the identified patient and the family through both child and family goals, while the discharge index was constructed on such principles. (For further explanation, see Horovitz-Darby, 1991.) Although there were many youth who failed this approach, more than not, many succeeded through this pathway. The proof was not only in those victorious youngsters who made developmental, educational, maturational, and therapeutic gain, but also in the pioneering administrators who convinced various arms of the governmental bureaucracy to fund such programs.

Led by a TQM (Total Quality Management) atmosphere which is governed on the principle of continuous drive toward quality care and commitment, as well as a milieu treatment approach, which incorporates a variety of programs and specialized therapies including psychotherapy, art therapy, dance therapy, music therapy, recreational therapy, occupational therapy, educational therapy, psychologic and psychiatric testing, medical treatment, sex education, substance abuse counseling, horticultural therapy, and continuous staff development training, just to mention a few, the agency was once the sixth largest of its kind in the United States. The reason behind its blossoming was myriad: the brilliance of the grant writers who created the programs; the commitment and earnest caring of the staff that implemented these programs; as well as the creativity of the administrators, who both honored and understood the necessity of valuing all of the arts of life. Unfortunately, financial constraints have changed the liberty of that functioning and some of the aforementioned specialized therapies are no longer offered at this agency. (So much for Health Maintenance Organizations.)

Although this agency is no longer so fortified, it stands apart in its pioneering methods and has provided an inspiring example for the future. I feel lucky to have been a part of such spirit. By no means was this agency panacean, rather it was adaptive, open, changing and flexible. And like the "flexible therapist," for the people who work there, it offered a climate, which bred commitment, loyalty, happiness via empowerment (rare in the workplace), growth, spirit, and above all, a place for the most wearied of characters, the soul. Do not mistake this for advertisement and false promotion. For it is not. Prior to my sojourn at this agency, I roamed from job to job, seeking an administrative succor, which believed in creativity, continuous education of its staff, and challenge. Until, I found this haven, I flitted from place to place, never sated or inspired long enough to stay.

The key element, which attracted my stay was in the word "challenge."

The artist in me begs for continuous exploration that accepts no boundaries. Finding that in one's work is a key factor that, in fact, frees the soul. Without such surroundings, the soul grows barren and withers away. I have found that in order to resonate with my patients on a spiritual level, my *own* spirit needs to be coddled by an ambience of genuine care, supervision, and freedom. (By now the reader is probably humming the bar, "I found my freedom on Blueberry Hill.")

But all jesting aside, I was truly lucky. As McNiff (1992) so eloquently stated in his treatise, *Art as Medicine,* we need to recognize the contributing factors of the pathological workplace that advances the erosion of the soul. And in fact, this should be applicable not only in mental health agencies but also in the corridors of the business world, which have also alienated and stifled the soul. If enterprise incorporated the soul, I wonder how pervasive depression would be amongst workers? One need only look at the staggering statistics on depression so commonplace among the laborers of the United States. Surely, the data reveals that something is fundamentally wrong here.

Moore (1992) underscored this phenomenon in his superb book, *Care of the Soul. A Guide for Cultivating Depth and Sacredness in Everyday Life.* It doesn't take a genius to look at the core of our society and be reminded of the fall of the Roman Empire. The question is, can we change the weft, rip out the mistake, and repair the damage before it is too late? And more basically, are we willing as a society to try?

## A NEW DIAGNOSIS

One need only look at the topics spearheading the best-sellers list to recognize this desperate cry for change. No longer are people willing to settle and ignore their collective unconscious. Instead, humankind is searching the vast wasteland, seeking answers, cures, miracles, when, in fact, isn't it as close as one's own backyard? But finally, even the community of psychiatry has taken the tantamount step of accepting the importance of the soul as stated in a recent article in *The New York Times* (Steinfels, 1994). At long last! Psychiatry now acknowledges a specific diagnosis for "Religious or Spiritual Problem(s)." This new diagnosis reflects "psychiatry's steady movement away from an earlier tendency to treat religion as a delusion or as evidence of immaturity, escapism and neurosis" (Steinfels, 1994). Instead, both religion and spirituality have been cast in a new light that no longer ignores these concerns nor interprets these questions as necessarily psychotic. Alas, the time finally has arrived for classifying this disorder in its proper context. In utilizing this diagnosis, the practitioner is urged to consider the possibility of a religious and/or spiritual problem. Unlike years ago, when a person was indeed often labeled "psychotic" and injected with psychotropics, now the movement is towards appropriate diagnosis, and hopefully, beneficial treatment and counseling:

V62.62 Religious or Spiritual Problem

This category can be used when the focus of clinical attention is a religious or spiritual problem. Examples include distressing experiences that involve loss or questioning of faith, problems associated with conversion to a new faith, or questioning of other spiritual values which may not necessarily be related to an organized church or institution.

(*Diagnostic and Statistical Manual of Mental Disorders,* 1994)
(Steinfels, 1994)

Nevertheless, psychiatry has not turned its back on truly delusional thinking. Rest assured, the diagnosis, which classifies such genuine psychosis, still exists. Yet perhaps the placement of this new disorder, V62.61, deserves some special explanation. On the one hand, I applaud the psychiatric community for recognizing this timely outcry and acknowledging that this struggle can coexist without necessarily courting psychosis. However, **by placing this classification in the V code category,** it is **not** an **insurable** diagnosis; that is, one cannot receive third-party reimbursements if this becomes the primary diagnosis. Instead, if a clinician expects remuneration for his services, this *cannot* be the primary diagnosis. Conversely, it exists in the hallway of other such V-code describers such as "Parent-Child Problem" (V61.20) or "Marital Problem" (V61.10).

*So*, in order to treat a patient who in fact has this problem, this cannot appear on an insurance claim form and extract monetary compensation for services.

What a paradox! The psychiatric profession *finally admits* the need to care for the soul *yet purposely* places this diagnosis in a category that for all intents and purposes is destined to remain forever untreated. Which is not to say, that treatment can't be done. Instead, the true diagnosis will have to hide behind a classification such as "Adjustment Disorder, with mixed disturbance of emotions and conduct" (309. 40). How unfitting. One step forward, and one step backward.

Perhaps this is Psychiatry's own *rhythmic disorder* which can only beat to the drum of the age old conflict, approach-avoidance. Like Sigmund Freud, the founding father of the psychiatric profession, religious and/or spiritual problems are still relegated to the position of a comforting illusion (imparted by our nuclear forebears, Mom and Pop) that a *mature* person eventually outgrows. Now, if that's not a contributing factor toward agnosticism, atheism, and continual confusion, I don't know what is! Still, the V-code classification is a beginning. But for those of us who are verily spiritually minded in our professional aspirations, clearly much educational work remains.

But let us now look at the results of the BATA on two very different types of emotionally disturbed youngsters in residential treatment. Although both were placed in a residential treatment facility, their questioning of God and spirituality impacted their treatment in very different ways. The first subject, a 14-year-old girl named Melissa, struggled with her relationship with God and involved Him in her recovery and spiritual direction. The second subject, an 18-year-old boy named Gary, sought God for the purpose of punishment and self-abasement. These two very different adolescents highlight the manner in which data extracted from the BATA can impact both assessment and the resulting treatment.

## MELISSA: A CASE FOR V62.61

In the early stages of my researching the BATA, Melissa, then 14.6, was referred to the Art Therapy Department for assessment and possible treatment. Her responses were peppered with themes portraying a deep-seated conflict about God. As a result, it was recommended by the administrant (another art therapist on staff) that she forego one more battery, the BATA. This suggestion was made in order to ascertain how her spiritual and religious thinking might impact her ability to mourn her losses and overcome her underlying anger and central depression.

Initially, some of the data, which led to the request, will be examined in order to clarify when such a petition should be granted. Although the tests administered, KFD (Burns & Kaufman, 1972), the HTP (Buck, 1950), and the SDT (Silver, 1992) revealed a variety of factors, including dissociation, enmeshment, lack of boundaries, low self-esteem, depression, and displacement within the family construct, the CATA (Horovitz-Darby, 1988) revealed a general questioning of Melissa's belief system. The Cognitive Art Therapy Assessment (CATA) unveiled Melissa's conflict with God and family dynamics.

The CATA sometimes can be amongst the most satisfactory of tests or in extreme cases, apt to generate the most anxiety. The reason is that there is no directive other than to create anything using the media: drawing, painting, and clay. The patient is allowed to choose the order in which these are produced and is permitted ample time to complete all three media. Oftentimes, this evaluation can extend beyond several appointments, depending on the person's investment in the process and end product (if there is one). Again, the reason might be twofold: (1) sheer enjoyment of the process whether through true, ego gratification and/or the concomitant freedom of regression and, (2) the releasing of inner tensions due to the nature of the nondirective component of the exercise.

When a client is particularly adverse to the traditional aforementioned batteries, it is suggested that the art therapist proceed directly with the CATA. More often than not, this examination yields cooperation and data. As well, once this section is completed, frequently the patient assents to additional testing. The reason for the continued testing is not only to reveal more data, but more importantly, to compare the findings and draw conclusions based on corresponding results.

## THE RESULTS OF THE CATA

Melissa gravitated toward the paint and displayed a propensity for working in masses. Although her thinking was concrete and suggested both cognitive deficits as well as perceptual pathology, the art seemed to unleash her capacity for ego gratification. Her painting revealed her current struggle with her overdue menarche and simultaneous stunted puberty (due to physical complications). (See genogram and timelines of both these cases at the conclusion of this chapter in order to glean the psychosocial picture of these youth.)

A mermaid, with bright red hair and fins, sits upon a rock. Melissa identified the mermaid as Ariel, the well-known character from the animated, Disney movie, "The Little Mermaid." The tale is about a young girl's discord as she transitions from childhood to adolescent sexuality. The mermaid, half human and half fish, may mirror Melissa's ambivalence of being half child and half adolescent. Melissa's manner in relating the story expressed a wish that her biological father save her and help her through this dilemma. In real life, however, her diabetic father is both unwilling and unable to help her. The additional characters of supportive father on the beach and evil sea witch in the underwater house seemed to also reflect the analogous feelings of the good and evil aspects of her father and estranged mother respectively. Additionally, Melissa painted a colossal Ariel between her father and Eric, the desired prince. Although this grandiose figure might propose narcissism, more accurately, it seems to echo Melissa's overcompensation for her short stature. Furthermore, the young prince appears to be idealized if not deified. He hovers over the water, arms outstretched, reminiscent of the parable of Christ walking on water (Figure 6-1).

Melissa's drawing response revealed a very interesting product. The work depicted a "smiling God on a cross" (Figure 6-2). Of interest is the opposite expression portrayed so obviously on this Christ figure. This rendition is not smiling but in fact quite apparently frowning. When the administrant inquired about her religious upbringing, she responded that she was raised Catholic and that she often attended church with her father. She added that she "(liked) God, because God feels good about Himself" and thus enabled her to "feel good about (herself)." Her next association was to create a clay Easter Bunny, a subject closely linked to the high holiday of Easter, and Christ's ascension into Heaven. Nevertheless, she had great difficulty forming this object, reflecting her struggle with forgiveness and atonement. With the art therapist's assistance, she was able to articulate the Easter Bunny, However, the resulting rabbit looked hostile and depressed. She commented that the buckteeth looked "like fangs." The hare was accompanied by the proverbial Easter basket filled with eggs and carrots, an obvious association to both nurturance and sexuality.

The previous drawing portion (Figure 6-2) invoked a great deal of anxiety. Melissa rushed through this section as quickly as possible. In the picture of "God on a cross," she first detailed a smile but later, Melissa decided to change His expression to a frown. Furthermore, she added tears, indicating a

Figure 6-1. Melissa's mermaid (CATA painting).

fundamental ambivalence regarding both her internal and external belief systems. When she was questioned about the tears, she responded that "God (was) crying because He's on the cross." This may support Melissa's need for denial, her concrete, operational thinking, or religious and/or spiritual preoccupation. Either way, the results reflected religious questionings and ambivalent posture regarding her belief system. In an effort to clarify these elements and determine whether or not a spiritual approach to Melissa's treatment would be, in fact, restorative and salutary, it was decided that the BATA be administered.

## THE BATA RESULTS

Initially, Melissa was reticent to answer the questions in a forthright manner. On the contrary, her responses were curt and deliberately abrupt. Within time, Melissa warmed up and her retorts were more genuine and thoughtful.

The first few questions were answered in a taciturn manner. She responded that she was Catholic, had attended church regularly in the past, and cur-

Figure 6-2. Melissa's smiling God on cross (CATA #2).

rently visited when offered an opportunity. When I inquired about any religious practices that she found meaningful, she seemed confused. She didn't
understand what I meant by "religious practices." As a result, I had to adjust
my questioning to her level of thinking. By doing so, I was able to determine
that she found receiving "God's bread" (the communion wafer) to be particularly significant as well as praying before bedtime and mealtime.

When queried further, Melissa revealed that she felt "secure, because (she
knew) God [was] up above." In watching over her, she firmly believed that
He would "not let anything happen" to her. Without any prodding, she then
stated, "I believe in God." She added that she had "already asked Him into
[her] heart." When I dialogued with her further, she explained one time when
she "went to church . . . it's like something in a weird way. . . . I kind of prayed
for Him to be in my heart." When I asked if that helped her somehow, she
replied, "Yeah. He's still in there."

In an effort to rule out pathology, I asked her to elaborate. She ascertained, "When I'm upset, I can hear Him saying, 'Calm down. Everything is going to be okay.' So I try to calm down." In embellishing further, Melissa commented that God made her feel strong and that she derived meaning from this. When asked to define exactly how God provided this for her, Melissa stated, "He tells me not to worry about anything because he watches over my family and me." Now at this point, one would wonder about Melissa's contention that God, in fact, *speaks* to her and per force dwells in her heart. While some might rule out a spiritual or religious component in favor of florid, psychotic thinking, I wondered more about the *nature* of this relationship and in what way it *served* her needs, positively or negatively. So I asked her what kinds of things she worried about. She very quickly responded that she worried about seeing her father and the fear that he would die from severe diabetes. She discussed a time when she had witnessed her father in a diabetic coma and how frightening that was for her. She then stated that she was learning to "trust God and other people." Indeed, the subject of trust caused Melissa to physically spill her drink and served to heighten her anxious state.

As soon as the art materials were provided, Melissa seemed more relaxed and occasionally blurted out her thoughts about God. For example, while working on the first directive and forming a heart-shaped container adorned with a crucifix and Jesus, she matter-of-factly stated, "God is always there when I need Him. If I'm upset or something he's just there and I can talk to Him. Just like I can talk to my toys. I have a Little Pony. If I'm upset, I can just talk to it and it listens; it may not talk back but it listens to me. In the same way, when I pray to God, He listens and helps me with my problems." (This clarified her use of imaginary play objects and her relationship with God as akin to that of a very young child's thinking.) While certainly not magical, as outlined in the above statements, it clearly smacked of developmental delays. She later stated that the heart-shaped box adorned with the Christ figure was extremely important to her because it was a "sign of love" (see Figure 6-3).

The second directive yielded a "buck-toothed devil" (Figure 6-4), which reminded me of her Easter Bunny response on the CATA clay subtest. She described this figure as being ugly and evil. Although Melissa had neither witnessed God nor its opposite (the devil) in the manner in which she had created them, she seemed genuinely pleased with the results and had difficulty ending the session.

The results of the test revealed Melissa's thinking to be concrete and developmentally delayed. As stated above, her internal belief system allowed her to utilize God in a redeeming manner. This coping mechanism was in fact prophylactic in nature. Like the thinking of a very young child, it provided Melissa with a much needed buffer when confronted with not only the harsh realities of her family life but also the teasing that she was subjected to due to

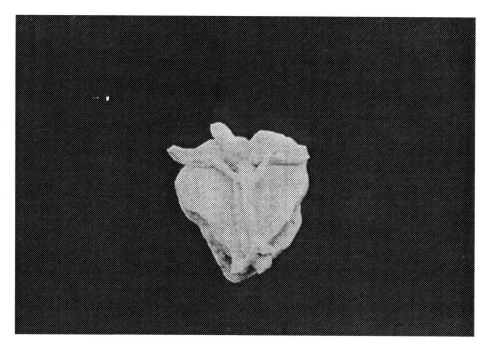

Figure 6-3. Melissa's BATA (1st directive).

her stunted physical stature. Moreover, while her external belief system warranted further exploration of her family of origin issues, the information revealed from the BATA justified Melissa's need for spiritual acceptance. As well, it outlined for the treatment team and her art therapist, the need to embrace her spiritual and religious dialogue and not to dismiss its content or remedial consequence. This information was pivotal in her treatment, as prior to the assessment, the psychiatrist was considering her banter concerning God to be predictive of florid, psychotic thinking. Yet, when the BATA results were shared, her diagnosis was changed and moreover, her length of stay was shortened. Clearly, here was a case where utilizing Melissa's religiosity as part of her treatment was beneficial to treatment, recovery, and eventual discharge from residential placement.

## GARY: SPIRITUAL CONSIDERATIONS

Gary, an agreeable 18-year-old adolescent young man, suffered from profound social, emotional, and developmental difficulties. His diagnosis of "autistic psychopathology," also known as Asperger's syndrome, has been

Figure 6-4. Melissa's BATA devil (2nd directive).

characterized by social isolation and eccentric behavior. Additional aspects which specifically defined Gary's attributes were: clumsy social approach, large and unwieldy gestures, lack of empathy, poor eye contact, little ability to form or maintain friendships, long-winded and often incoherent speech patterns, and bizarre preoccupations.

Gary's thinking was extremely concrete, circular, perseverative, and effusive. Moreover, he appeared to be functioning at the level of a two- or three-year-old child. Although able to differentiate between reality and fantasy, his associations were often tangential and quite bizarre.

Gary's family life was extremely chaotic. (See genogram and timeline at end of this chapter.) He had been neglected and physically abused by his mother until the age of two. Both his mother and father were described as alcohol and drug dependent. As a result, at his age of two, Gary and his one-year-old sister were surrendered by his parents and adopted by his paternal grandparents. This adoptive family and his half-siblings (who were in actuality his aunts and uncles) ostracized Gary, casting him into the role of scapegoat and the identified patient. Frequently, his adoptive father-grandfather physically and verbally abused him. Gary's response to this treatment often took the form of suicidal gesturing. On more than one occasion, Gary attempted to hang himself.

One of his sibling-aunts (age 23) shared a bedroom with Gary and behaved in a sexually provocative manner. It was suspected that she had in fact sexually abused Gary. Often he spied on this sibling-aunt and watched her through a vent in the adjacent room. Previous inappropriate sexual behavior had also been reported: there had been allegations that Gary had molested several younger school boys in addition to his six and one-half year-old half-sister (biological father's daughter from a second marriage).

At Gary's age 14, the sister with whom he had shared a bedroom moved out of the home. His response was to insert a sewing needle into his urethra. Several months later when she returned home, Gary again implanted a four inch needle in his penis, which had to be surgically removed. At this point, he entered residential treatment.

Because of his social inadequacies and maladaptive behavior, Gary was quickly out of favor with his peers. As a result, he openly masturbated, chewed on his toes and on occasion inappropriately touched the genitalia of another resident. Unable to curb his physiologic impulses, Gary was often placed under adult surveillance in order to prevent him from acting on his sexual impulses, harming others or himself. His obsession with self-abusive behavior became so flagrantly out of control that at one point he was in danger of losing his toes because of an infection from this oral aggressive, self-harming behavior.

Clearly, he was a very disturbed teenager with limited social skills and resources. Nevertheless, he was cooperative in art therapy treatment and developed a formidable therapeutic alliance with his art therapist (Elyse Capell). He was able to disclose his depression, underlying anger, and suicidal ideation while in art therapy sessions. Moreover, he was able to utilize the materials appropriately and sublimated his anger and anxiety by redirecting those feelings appropriately onto the art materials. This modality also heightened his sense of self-worth. At times, this amplified sense of self fell subject to grandiosity, but for the most part, it served his needs in a more socially acceptable manner.

As he continued in treatment, general themes of isolation and impoverishment moved towards his need to construct reality. Although this new direction was tempered with bits of grandiosity and an overall hypervigilance, some of his noxious habits were slowly dissipating: for example, although still isolated by his peer residents, he was no longer a scapegoat amongst his peers and his self-harming behavior had subsided. Even his toes improved.

Still, since Gary had never developed a relationship with an idealized image (e.g., a positive mother introject) and as Kohut (1977) would offer, had not developed a network for affectionate mirroring or basic need for self, he was incapable of relying on any kind of internal locus of control. Per force, he responded to an external locus of control. His artwork reflected this depression and his verbal associations suggested that he felt completely unchecked and in fact possessed by an external force, the devil. Kohut (1977) referred to these preoccupations and inability for self-regulation as directly related to narcissistic trauma and lack of integration. Verily, Gary was a product of an environment that inculcated this response.

Because Gary had brought up his feelings about God and the devil repeatedly in treatment, as Elyse's supervisor, I suggested asking Gary if he were willing to take the BATA in order to investigate this aspect, which seemed to manacle his growth and treatment. He agreed. Unfortunately, Elyse felt uncertain about conducting this new assessment and so instead, I administered the test while she watched and videotaped the session.

A few things occurred that neither of us had taken into account and I mention them here because we learned them through our mistake: Primarily, even though Gary knew me fairly well and we had a cordial relationship, Elyse should have executed the test. In hindsight, neither of us had considered Gary's need to impress me and tailor his responses in what might have been a saccharine nature. Elyse, in fact, was genuinely surprised by some of his responses and believed that his rejoinder might have been influenced by his desire to please me and be accepted. Strangely enough, we had not considered this since I had been familiar with Gary for approximately three years. Big mistake.

Secondly, we had not accounted for Gary's response to being videotaped because he had been taped in the past. But this time, we were dealing with belief systems and it kicked up all kinds of associations to authority figures and punishment; as a result, Gary continually turned to the camera and implored his "mother" to see what a "good boy" he was. Although this was fascinating material, we had discounted Gary's voyeuristic tendencies and the effect that the camera would have on him. Yet, it certainly conjured up rich material. Here again, had we used our one-way mirror for observation, the results might have been colored differently.

So to put it bluntly, we were not certain whether or not the situation biased the results. Again, had the players been different, perhaps we would have obtained a less skewed response. It's difficult to predict and there is no way that we will know. Yet after this experience, I definitely feel that the assessment should *only* be conducted by the practitioner who is *directly* involved in the case. Clinically, it makes more sense. Live and learn. But here are the results from this very interesting case.

## THE BATA: GARY

Gary stated that he was a Nazarene Christian and stated that he attended a Nazarene church. Since I was unfamiliar with whether or not this was true, I had no reason to discount it. Yet Elyse was completely unaware of such an affiliation. Furthermore, when I questioned how often he attended church, he stated twice weekly. It then became moot since he proffered that he attended the services at the treatment center. His nebulous responses continued as he stated that he had a relationship with the staff minister. Here, I became completely confused since he didn't know the accurate name of the staff priest.

When I asked the more esoteric questions, such as, "What kind of relationship do you have with God?" Gary honed in on his more intrinsic feelings. For example, he responded, "I have a good relationship with Him. He gives us eternal life as much as possible. We forgive us our sins to Him. I understand that He loves me."

So even though he had twisted some of the maxims, his concept of forgiveness, acceptance and understanding was quite established. When asked to extrapolate, he explained that the reason that his relationship with God was good was because every time he did something "sinful," he had to do something good. And if he were "disrespectful" to Him, then that, too, would constitute sin. He added that he tried to err on the positive side.

His response to what gave him strength and meaning in his life offers the reader a semblance of Gary's enormous guilt and shame: "Good behavior is good strength. . . . He forgives me for doing things that I do wrong. And then I say, 'Please forgive me. Oh God; I've done something badly. Please forgive me my sins and I hope that I be your faithful servant, your trusted, your very trusted servant.' And, I always do that. I always say that to Him."

As he started the first task, he became generally uncomfortable and expressed how "complicated" he felt the process was. After a bit of inquiry, I learned that this "complication" hinged on his discomfort with the video camera. Moreover, he stated, "My mom is going to be . . . well, I hope my mom understands that . . . I hope I do a good job here once I leave here." When I asked him if he worried about doing a good job once he left the agency, he admittedly acknowledged his concerns. Moreover, Gary also expressed concerns about doing a "good job" at home and fears about his mother's opinion.

His picture, 6-5, depicts him kneeling by his bed, wearing a cross, and praying to God at night. Interestingly enough, this crucifix image came up repeatedly post-test, so most likely it triggered a novel response in Gary. He explained, "I've just drawn nighttime. . . . I always pray to Him every night. So then I can understand what I'm feeling and what I have done, what I've really done. I should actually start doing." When I asked Gary to clarify what he meant, he explained that he felt the need to "pray more" in order to have a better idea of why he had "done the things [he] had done." He clarified that he felt "God could help [him] with that." About his picture, Gary was able to articulate that he felt good about God and himself, and that he had witnessed God like that.

Figure 6-5. Gary praying to God.

Again, while setting up for the second directive, Gary stated to the camera, "You know, I'm really a nice man, you see. I really like doing this. This fun type of stuff, you know. I'm really into this." Clearly, Gary was experiencing discomfort whether because of his association to the testing and/or being videotaped. When I mirrored his concern about someone thinking that perhaps he wasn't nice, he readily confessed his obsession with his mother's opinion.

So perhaps association to his mother was engendered by the subject matter of the testing, the *ultimate authority figure,* God. In fact this was verified later when Elyse and I questioned him further about his picture and his mother's effect on his relationship with God. At first, Gary responded rather defensively: "No, she doesn't do that at all! She never does that at all. We have . . . we never have rules in the house. We can't wear crosses in our religion at all. My sister does that but we don't have a rule like that." Moreover, while emphasizing his need to "follow God's laws," we inquired about what would happen if he didn't follow God's laws.

Gary elucidated, "I'd be in danger. . . . I would get punished for my actions. . . . I would get punished for doing things that were wrong." Elyse boldly asked, "Your mother would punish you?" To which, Gary meekly replied, "Yes." From there, we were able to help Gary connect his mother to his perspective of God as a "punishing" God. Stories were then relayed about his past behavior, including stealing. With that admission, I was able to connect Gary's obsession with perfection as directly related to his guilt and desire for atonement. In dialoguing about his need to feel forgiveness from God, I was able to help Gary link this need for self-forgiveness.

In the second directive (Figure 6-6), Gary was unable to create God's opposite. Instead, he detailed "God's son." This picture illustrated the move to Egypt due to the evil King Herod's proclamation to kill the newborn king of the Jews. He explained that this was Jesus' house and that his mother was "inside" the house (perhaps establishing the locus of control that Gary so lacked). He further explained that King Herod was "the evil one."

When Gary was asked if he had ever experienced the evil of King Herod in his own life, he suggested, "Everybody said they did not like Herod. They wished they had a new king, so they did. I don't feel evil like Herod did back then." So when I inquired how he felt about what he had made, he responded, "I feel lucky. I feel nice today. I feel great. I feel wonderful. . . . That I do some things right."

According to Anechiarico (1990) and Gilby, Wolf and Goldberg (1989), adolescents, like Gary, whose needs are unsatisfied and are not patterned with a powerful self-object for internalization and identification, become prematurely disillusioned and instead identify with isolated, sexualized, voyeuristic preoccupations. Furthermore, the striving of the self breaks down and often results in sexualized, exhibitionistic behavior. Optimally, aiding the development of an internal locus of control fosters socially adaptive behavior while simultaneously counteracting impulsivity, delay of gratification, and grandiose, exhibitionistic thoughts.

According to his therapist, Elyse Capell (1991), Gary had been "empowered through a nondirective approach to art therapy" (p. 17). Additionally, he was able to extract an internal locus of control by formulating, achieving, and mastering his own goals via the art materials. As therapy progressed, he demonstrated "increasing pride in his work and evidence[d] fewer manifestations of depression, both visually and verbally" (p. 17). Of significance was his decreased preoccupation with devils and demons, which he believed had previously controlled his behavior. Although art therapy was not an elixir, it certainly provided Gary with the mechanism to explore his fantasies in a proscribed and safe environment, establish an avenue for promoting self esteem, and most importantly enact a therapeutic alliance in order to locate his missing piece—the self.

Cataloguing the information deduced from the BATA amplified the necessity of staying the journey toward an internal locus of control. Although Ms. Capell had clearly traversed that pathway prior to the assessment, the BATA reinforced and provided her with the additional fodder to reverse the damage and chart the passage towards spiritual recovery.

Figure 6-6. Gary's God's son.

## CONCLUSIONS ABOUT THE CASES

Although the BATA was introduced in the first case at the inception of treatment and in the latter case approximately two months before discharge, the resulting data revealed information about the spiritual dimensions of each case and allowed for application either to expand the treatment process and/or amplify it.

In the first case, religiosity was be ruled out as a predictor of pathology and instead, Melissa's need for spiritual acceptance was given its place in treatment. In the second case of Gary, the information, educed from the BATA, reinforced his art therapist's treatment protocol and underscored her direction in treatment.

The two cases presented herein outlined varying levels of disturbance. Indisputably, the overriding factor of incorporating a spiritual dimension into assessment, diagnosis, and treatment contributed to results that influenced the course of treatment in both patients. Indeed, the information extracted from the BATA assessment not only provided an increased understanding of belief/faith/cultural systems, but more importantly enhanced familial information, produced efficacy of treatment, and revealed yet another avenue for communication. While, the data had varying applications, the information yielded pathways to the spirit and the soul. And is this not our task?

MELISSA

C.A. 14.6
D.O.B. 09/02/78

White female, short, plump, dark curly hair.
Talkative, eager to please. No sex abuse.
Allegations of possible aggravated physical abuse
perpetrated by father. No known substance abuse.
Withdrawn, anxious, depressed, rage, angry
outbursts, low self-esteem.

■ SUICIDE IDEATION/GESTURES

injured father in angry outburst

poor impulse control

exposed self in school: touched genitalia
in class & smelled and licked fingers afterwards

touched boy's genitalia

disclosed touching mother's ex-boyfriend's
genitalia once

poor attention span

poor social skills, few friends, often scapegoated

hoards food, sometimes overeats

threatened father with scissors

held knife to own stomach

poor in academics, family moved a lot
and changed schools

disturbed by family problems

afraid of father dying

distrustful of others and environment

fights with siblings

oppositional

somewhat histrionic

Medication

currently on Prozac, 20 mg daily
to improve impulse control and
control angry outbursts.

tried Mellaril, Lithium, Imiprimine,
Clonidine & Pamelor all with
mixed results or none

Physical Health

good except for wandering left eye

head injury in 1987

delayed onset of puberty

short, but growing at normal rate

allergic to penicillin

Strengths

motivated for treatment

enjoys arts/crafts, sports

talks about personal issued & feelings

disturbed about family problems

Nightmares, fear of thunder; doctors

anxious about future

somewhat histrionic

no thought disorder

Mother

white, employed, separated,
medical technician

at one point abandoned
daughters and lived with
son and boyfriend

unmotivated

Father

white, unemployed

diabetic, very ill

motivated about treatment

cannot control Melissa

comes to family sessions

possibly physically abused Melissa

Melissa's Genogram

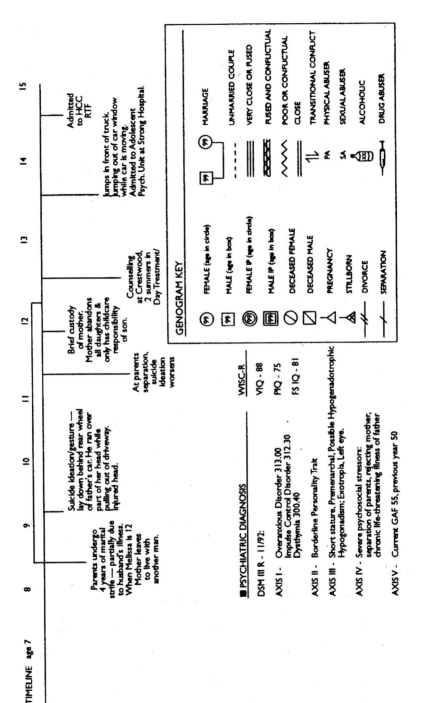

TIMELINE   age 7    8      9      10     11     12     13     14     15

Parents undergo 4 years of marital strife — partially due to husband's illness. When Melissa is 12 Mother leaves to live with another man.

Suicide Ideation/gesture — lay down behind rear wheel of father's car. He ran over part of her head while pulling out of driveway. Injured head.

Brief custody of mother. Mother abandons all daughters & only has childcare responsibility of son.

At parents separation, suicide ideation worsens

Counselling at Crestwood, 2 summers in Day Treatment/

Jumps in front of truck. Jumping out of car window while car is moving. Admitted to Adolescent Psych. Unit at Strong Hospital.

Admitted to HCC RTF

**■ PSYCHIATRIC DIAGNOSIS**

DSM III R - 11/92:

AXIS I - Overanxious Disorder 313.00
         Impulse Control Disorder 312.30
         Dysthymia 300.40

AXIS II - Borderline Personality Trait

AXIS III - Short stature, Premenarchal, Possible Hypogenadotrophic Hypogonadism; Exotropia, Left eye.

AXIS IV - Severe psychosocial stressors; separation of parents, rejecting mother, chronic life-threatening illness of father

AXIS V - Current GAF 55, previous year 50

WISC-R

VIQ - 88

PIQ - 75

FS IQ - 81

GENOGRAM KEY

(99)  FEMALE (age in circle)        (99)  MARRIAGE

[99]  MALE (age in box)

(99⊙)  FEMALE IP (age in circle)    [99]—(99)  UNMARRIED COUPLE

[99]  MALE IP (age in box)          ══════  VERY CLOSE OR FUSED

⊘  DECEASED FEMALE                  ══════  FUSED AND CONFLICTUAL

☒  DECEASED MALE                    ∿∿∿∿  POOR OR CONFLICTUAL

△  PREGNANCY                        ═══  CLOSE

▲  STILLBORN                        ⇅  TRANSITIONAL CONFLICT

╱  DIVORCE                          PA  PHYSICAL ABUSER

╱  SEPARATION                       SA  SEXUAL ABUSER

                                    ⊠  ALCOHOLIC

                                    ⊟  DRUG ABUSER

Melissa's Timeline

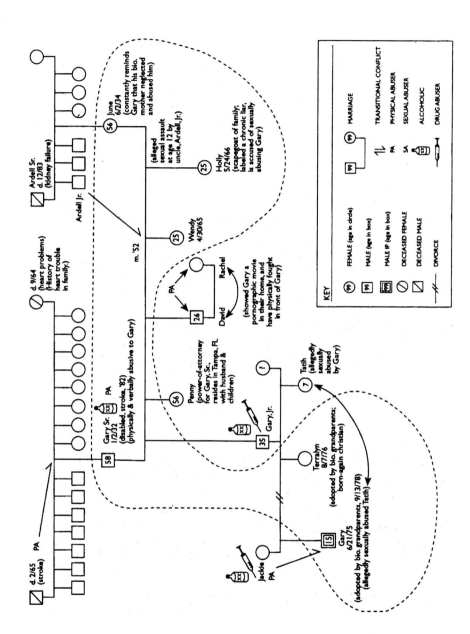

Gary's Genogram

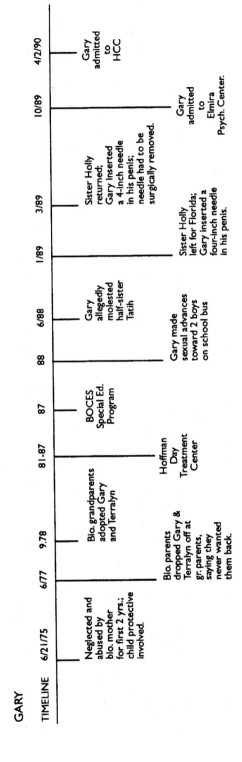

GARY

| TIMELINE | 6/21/75 | 6/77 | 9.78 | 81-87 | 87 | 88 | 6/88 | 1/89 | 3/89 | 10/89 | 4/2/90 |
|---|---|---|---|---|---|---|---|---|---|---|---|

Neglected and abused by bio. mother for first 2 yrs.; child protective involved.

Bio. parents dropped Gary & Terralyn off at gr. parents, saying they never wanted them back.

Bio. grandparents adopted Gary and Terralyn

Hoffman Day Treatment Center

BOCES Special Ed. Program

Gary made sexual advances toward 2 boys on school bus

Gary allegedly molested half-sister Tatih

Sister Holly left for Florida; Gary inserted a four-inch needle in his penis.

Sister Holly returned; Gary inserted a 4-inch needle in his penis; needle had to be surgically removed.

Gary admitted to Elmira Psych. Center.

Gary admitted to HCC

Gary's Timeline

# Chapter 7

# THE SPIRITUAL TREATMENT OF
# A SUICIDAL BULIMIC ANORECTIC

Those who do not find time to exercise will have to find time for illness.

—The Earl of Derby, 1873

Mind, Body, and Spirit" (John 17:21). As long as I can remember, this statement has been the national logo for the YMCA. I have passed it while swimming laps in their pool and pondered its meaning while lifting weights on the Nautilus machines. Emotionally, physically, and spiritually, I have meditated on this proverb and I have come to believe in its truth and inner direction towards a life of fullness, meaning, and wellness. It is such a simple thought yet so incredibly poignant. For one person, it can be medicinal and yet for others, it can be sadly misconstrued and injurious.

The case, which I am about to present, is that of a bulimic anorectic. Like others afflicted by this disease, Linda utilized exercise not as a prescription toward wellness but as an obsessive-compulsive mechanism that was employed for weight control. Moreover, the 1990s had been a time that emphasized health, exercise, fitness, youth, and unfortunately thinness. Yet exercise, despite its energy, contributed to this paradigm.

The endorphins released by the body during exercise are akin to the high one experiences on drugs. Because of this secondary gain, exercise in itself can be an addictive process. Personally, I have found that I, too, *need* exercise. These endorphins energize my mind, my body, and *most* of all my spirit. Without it, I often become unpleasant to be around. I am aware of both its positive and negative ramifications. Although Derby's quote, which opens up this chapter, is verily true, it can also contribute to one's destruction. In the case of Linda, *overexercising* was her undoing.

111

## PRESENTING SYMPTOMS AND PSYCHOSOCIAL HISTORY

Linda, a second generation, Italian Catholic, came to see me ten years before the writing of this case. At that time, she was 40 years old, married to a third generation, white Anglo-Saxon Protestant for 19 years, and had a 16-year-old son named Mitchell. (When she returned to therapy for the second time, ten years had elapsed. She was 50, her husband (Ted) was 51, and her son was 25.) (See genogram at the end of this chapter for complete psychosocial history.)

At Linda's age one, her sister, Jill, was born and contracted polio. As a result, Linda moved in with her grandmother, Angelica, for the next three years of her life. Being the firstborn grandchild had its rewards. Linda was cherished by this household, particularly by her childless, Aunt Nancy. Still, she felt displaced and rejected by her mother, Maria. During the next seven years, which preceded her mother's divorce from her father, Seth, she remembered countless arguments between her parents. When Seth finally left, he moved across the country. A brief reconciliation occurred several months later before Seth learned that Maria had an affair with the across-the-street neighbor, Cory. Soon after, he divorced Maria and married a younger woman also named Linda.

At this juncture, Linda's childhood was filled with terrible memories. She recounted stories of a chaotic, unkempt household where there were no fixed meals or bedtimes. Being the parentified child, she often cared for her sister, Jill (aged nine), and infant half-sister, Jane (born out of wedlock with Cory). Meanwhile, her mother cleaned other people's homes or took in sewing to make end's meet. Instead of healthy after-school snacks, the kitchen table was always strewn with pastries, Hostess Twinkies ©, and cakes. As a result, Linda learned very early to equate sugary food with love. (In fact, she could not recall receiving any physical affection from her mother. The only exception was when Linda gave birth to Mitchell; Maria hugged her upon visitation. Linda recalled "recoiling from (her) mother's grasp" as if she were a "venomous snake.")

Linda vividly recalled nightly jaunts across town to spy on Cory and his wife, Elaine. Maria would force the children to walk across town (a 45 minute excursion), sneak into the bushes, peak through the windows of Cory's other home, and recount the events to their mother. On other nights, Jane would often be dressed up and Cory would sneak up the back stairs of Maria's home and visit with his child. Perhaps this memory was the most painful for Linda since she struggled not only with her mother's out-of-wedlock relationship but the concurrent abandonment of her biological father. Indeed, raised in the Catholic schools (under the doctrines of Vatican I), Linda grew up believing she "would go to Hell" because her mother and father divorced. These church laws left a deleterious imprint on her spirit and ability as an adult to maintain a relationship with God.

Although Linda did not report any significant childhood diseases or abnormal medical history, much later during treatment, she recalled being sexually abused at age 10 by her Aunt Marjorie's husband, Colin (see genogram). Like other victims of sexual abuse, Linda often blocked memories of the abuse and seemed to be suffering from post-traumatic stress. When she could bring herself to disclose the abuse, she remembered two or three incidents. During the recalled molestation, she remembered her mother being in the yard below when Colin forced her into bed with him and fondled her genitalia and breasts. She could not recollect whether or not there had been vaginal penetration since she described this period in her life as "foggy." (The description she used seemed apt since dissociation often accompanies sexual abuse incidents.) Moreover, she was threatened by Colin to never disclose the incidents. And, she didn't, not to anyone, until treatment with me.

Ashamed of her background, she was determined to rise above her upbringing, managed to graduate summa cum laude, and became a doctor. (These facts she repeatedly emphasized throughout her treatment.) As well, she felt equally burdened by her low socio-economic class origin even though she had married into an upper class echelon.

Prior to medical school, she married Ted and a few years later begrudgingly bore him his only son. Upon her release from the hospital, Linda sank into a deep depression. From her description, she clearly had suffered from post-partum depression. Untreated, Linda was listless and remained bedridden while Ted cared for the baby. She described this period in her life as "awful" and felt that she had "sinned against God." According to Linda, her reasons were threefold: she neither had her marriage blessed nor her child baptized and she felt she had been abusive towards Mitchell, enforcing bedtimes, throwing him in his bed, and yelling at him to obey her command. Moreover, while Linda attended church regularly, she abstained from receiving the sacraments. She was convinced that she had committed a mortal sin and could not participate in this important ritual.

Although Mitchell grew up to be a decent, young man, Linda constantly chided herself for not being a better mother. Nevertheless, she forged a wonderful relationship with him during his adolescence.

However, when Mitchell developed Hepatitis B in his early twenties, she felt directly responsible since she had religiously administered antibiotics, which were prescribed for him as a child. Because he had suffered numerous earaches during his youth, this course of treatment intermittently spanned several years. Even though his disease was clearly related to alcoholic drinking, Linda was determined to blame herself, stating repeatedly that as a "doctor," she should have questioned the pediatrician instead of blindly following his advice. And when this disease miraculously left Mitchell's system, Linda still failed to see the connection between Mitchell's drinking and his disorder. She steadfastly insisted that *she* was the cause of his illness. She needed to be at fault and continually cast herself in the role of the identified patient. Yet to the outside world, she believed everyone perceived her as "perfect."

Her appearances became her *raison d'être*. She developed an eating disorder, which she hid from her family. Eight years before our treatment, she binged on sugary foods and ate until she practically passed out. Daily outings to the local supermarket resulted in hedonistic consumption while in her car. When she would allow herself the luxury of keeping a gallon of ice cream in her freezer, she would throw it out, only to retrieve it later from the garbage and devour it like a crazed animal. Not surprisingly, the onset of this disorder coincided with her husband's development of melanoma. Nevertheless, even when Ted went into remission and seemingly "beat the odds," Linda continued her bingeing.

When she first contacted me for an appointment, her eating disorder was in full swing and three weeks earlier, her husband became frustrated with her asexual behavior and had blackened her eye. This had been the first and only incident of violence in her 19 years of marriage. On intake, she and Ted were not speaking, but she resolutely denounced my idea of her husband accompanying her to treatment. In fact, she was so guarded about this other side of herself that she specifically sought my counseling **because** my practice was an hour's drive from her hometown.

Although she preferred to paint an idyllic picture of her husband's family system, his nuclear family was also beset with problems. His family's communication style was quite constricted and formal. As a result, his sister, Miriam, relied on alcohol and various drugs to help her cope with family pressures. Ted's younger brother, Bryant, was a closet homosexual until he contracted AIDS and died. At that time, Ted's parents' dependency on alcohol increased, as they attempted to drown their sorrows.

Linda's sister, Jill, resided in a Boston-style home, which was co-owned by her mother. Maria inhabited the upstairs apartment while Jill, her husband, and two daughters lived in the downstairs apartment. This made for uncomfortably close quarters and resulted in Jill's constant depression. Moreover, Jill suffered numerous psychiatric hospitalizations and repeated treatments of ECT (electroshock therapy). Jill, Jane, and the mother also reportedly struggled with food issues. Linda described her mother as "obese." Interestingly enough, neither Linda's sisters nor mother were aware of her eating disorder because she was so thin. She was considered "the *successful* one, the star, the one who made it."

## PARAMETERS OF THE PERSONALITY

Linda's appearance almost belied her condition. Although she was thin, she wore layers of clothing and by no means appeared anorectic. She was attractive, tall, conservatively well dressed, and rigidly composed. Her teeth and gums, however, revealed the telling characteristics of a bulimic anorectic: all of her teeth were capped. (This crossover symptomatolgy of alternate bingeing and fasting cycles is actually not an unusual condition.)

Linda's intractable compulsion to be viewed as a "star" and ascend toward perfection was her undoing. This pretense resulted in a mask mired in false disguises and behaviors. Her presentation was hampered by a saccharine facade; her demeanor suggested an approachable, engaging personality; and her posture seemed self-assured and confident. Yet underneath this exterior beat the heart and soul of an isolated, lonely, human being who cloaked herself in armor fabricated for the purpose of avoiding interaction, friendship, and relationships. Ironically, this was the apparel that she so desperately wanted to relinquish, yet dominated the crux of her treatment.

Linda's family of origin issues aptly fit the configurations described by various theorists: Bruch's (1973) identification of achievement-oriented families with domineering, rejecting mothers and characteristics as outlined by Minuchin, Rosman, and Baker (1978) also reflected Linda's posture: These features included enmeshment (with her son), poor conflict resolution (with her family of origin and her husband), and a propensity toward triangulation in familial relationships. Lubber also described the following profile that fit Linda's nature. These were "devotion to work; . . . depression; feelings of powerlessness; low self-esteem; . . . perfectionism; obsessive-compulsive behaviors; and a denial of (her) sexual self" (1991, p.58).

Bruch (1973) also purported a therapeutic stance that challenged erroneous thinking in order to facilitate recovery and alter cognitive distortions. Moreover, an anorectic's thinking seemed to be colored by extreme perceptions: As Lubber pointed out, "everything is perceived all black or all white" (1991, p. 61). There were no grays for an anorectic. Therefore the art tasks needed to encourage living in the gray in order to reframe this perspective.

## SIGNIFICANT SESSIONS

After gathering information on Linda, I suggested that she attempt to at least dialogue with her husband. When she next entered, she attempted to present a front of being "just fine" but within ten minutes, she sobbed uncontrollably. I suggested that she use clay to make whatever she wanted. (This directive is actually a subtest of the CATA (Cognitive Art Therapy Assessment) as published in Horovitz-Darby, 1988.) She repeatedly cut a hole in the clay and then filled it up. I gingerly interpreted this doing and undoing and gently suggested that perhaps her activity was synonymous to her eating disorder. She concurred and quickly created a small "blob" of clay, declaring it to be a self-portrait. She next created a small figure of her husband and expressed her ambivalence about confronting him. She admitted wanting to poison him. We role played the scenario and I suggested ways in which she could communicate with her husband without attacking and/or killing him and encourage further domestic abuse.

The next session she cheerfully reported that they had reconciled their differences. Much to my surprise, Linda had admitted that she was seeing a "marriage counselor." Although Ted offered to accompany her to treatment, Linda steadfastly refused him this opportunity. I explored her resistance and need to defend against increased intimacy.

Within a month, Linda had her eating "under control." Yet her methods worried me. She felt able to control her bingeing because of me. When she wasn't in my office, Linda viewed me as a "guardian angel watching over (her) shoulder." Such omnipotent comparisons were the first glimmers of not only positive transference but also deep-seated conflicts with God.

## A NOTE ON SUPERVISION AND RECORD KEEPING

Perhaps because I had not yet created the BATA, I had not made this connection directly in the therapeutic confines. Although somewhere inside me, I felt that she was unable to address her spiritual and religious conflicts. If I had been convinced that she could have handled this material, I might have at least brought it up. Instead, I diligently recorded these thoughts in my session notes, filed them in my clinical hat for later use, and renounced this opportunity to explore these concepts. As an alternative, I suggested her *inability* to credit herself and explored her *low self-esteem*.

However, here, I must add a thought for the reader: thanks to the guidance of past, great supervisors (Werner Halpern, MD; Lewis Ward, MD; Sybil Baldwin, ACSW, CSW, AAMFT; and Laurie Wilson, Ph.D., ATR-BC), I have **always** kept very extensive notes on my patients (complete with drawings, before the advent of digital photography) and in many instances, when permission was granted by the patient, videotaped sessions. Because of this record keeping, I have been able to utilize these "light bulb moments" in moving my clients towards wellness. While I also have auditory recall (sometimes much to my chagrin), I have always encouraged my students, interns, and supervisees to record therapeutic sessions in the same manner as described above. Even when one does not have the luxury of auditory recall or photographic memory, if a clinician merely rereads the previous session notes before each subsequent session, then the artwork produced in the previous session (left surreptitiously out on the art table) plus the clinician's "memory" can serve as a springboard to continue where the patient last left off. In my experience, this has proved to be quite efficacious in moving a patient more quickly and efficiently towards wellness. So to summarize, the *vantage* in using the verbal associates coupled with the artworks tools fosters **continuity between sessions.** And that is the difference between just *doing* therapy as opposed to being a *responsive, dedicated* clinician. I mention these notions *because* I had the privilege of great supervisors hammering this into me. I hope that this will promote the same in the reader.

## DIRECTIONS IN TREATMENT

Soon after that session, I recommended that Linda also attend a group for eating disorders: I felt the additional support of women with similar personality parameters might enhance her treatment. Although she was resistant, she complied. I soon learned that she felt *paralyzed* in the group, remained mute, and felt unable to disclose anything for several months. Here again was another surprise. Perhaps I had moved her too quickly towards group treatment. While I had thought that the group support would have engendered wellness, instead it crippled her.

This became another obstacle for her in treatment. She felt her problems to be insignificant when compared to those of the group members. Simultaneously, she was revolted by several of the group members: one sickened her because she was "so obese" and reminded her of her mother. Linda detested another member because she had the support of her mother and a spouse. (Nevertheless, this latter information aided my ability to discuss her resistance to disclosing her disorder to Ted and to begin to discuss family dynamics with her current nuclear family and family of origin.) I then suggested that she "draw herself and her family doing something" (the Kinetic Family Drawing (KFD) instruction as described by Burns and Kaufmann, 1972).

Her response, Figure 7-1, portrays Linda separated from her husband and son by a wall. The primitive rendering of the figures also suggests regression and anxiety associated with the family constellation. On the right, Linda is depicted with her back to the viewer preparing a meal in the kitchen. Her pets, two cats and a dog flank her. This perspective seems to reflect Linda's need to *literally* turn her back on her family. Instead, she appears more com-

Figure 7-1. Linda's KFD.

fortable relating to the family pets. Moreover, she views herself as subservient to the needs of her family and interestingly enough, illustrates herself as preparing a meal.

(However, after inquiring about the picture, I learned that Linda's family *never* engaged in routine meals. This cemented my ability to prescribe a plan to incorporate both family interaction and eating sensibly prepared meals together.)

To the left of Linda, she drew her husband and son prone on a couch and chair (respectively). They were both engaged in watching football on television and she described them as "couch potatoes" who had "everything in common." Clearly, her statement further underscored her view as isolated and alienated from this family system.

(Of interest is the topographical perspective of Ted and Mitchell. This bird's eye view suggests possible dissociation of feelings. As well, both Ted and Mitchell lack a mouth, suggesting Linda's inability to both nurture them (thus disclosing her inability to mother and care for her family) and sustain verbal communication.)

For the next few months, treatment issues revolved around Linda's view of herself as good or bad, perfect or imperfect. This was a woman who only saw

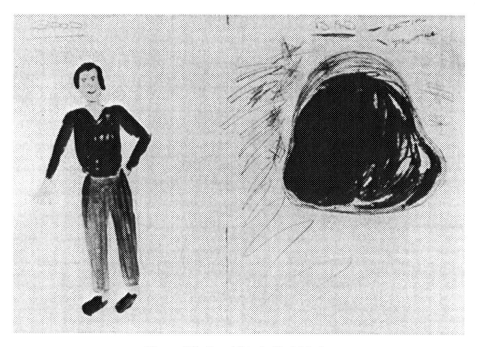

Figure 7-2. Good Linda/Bad Linda.

black and white. Living in the gray was utterly impossible for her. Figure 7-2 is representative of her work at this time.

Her left self-representation of the "good" Linda depicts her as upright and smiling. The stance, in reality, would cause her to topple over. Telling details suggest similar inconsistencies: the omission of ears point to her difficulty around communication with others; her red blouse and blue pants reflect conflicting emotions regarding bodily urges and issues (according to Alschuler and Hattwick, 1947). On the opposite side of the paper, Linda created her repetitive schema and trademark, "the blob," to represent her self image of the "bad" Linda. The words "eating" and "fighting" were listed next to "bad" as indices of her behavior that she found impossible to eliminate.

Continued sessions were marked by jagged crying spells. Three months later, she entered the office and proudly announced that she had finally spoken up during her group. This was followed by a binge the following week; I interpreted her bingeing as a need to distance herself from others, avoid parenting herself and significant others, and as a mechanism for remaining "sick" and connected to the other group members. Sadly, she concurred.

Linda went on holiday a few weeks later but when she returned, she discovered a half-gallon of ice cream left inside her freezer by her mother. Unable to control herself, she consumed the entire contents. She prattled on

about her mother and then mentioned an incident when Jane was newly
borne. When mother returned from the hospital, she displayed Jane to both
Jill and Linda. She recalled her mother earnestly saying, "Well, should we
keep her?" After this disclosure, Linda began to cry. When she stopped, I
asked her if she connected this to when she was given away (Jill's birth and
subsequent bout with polio). She denied this connection. So, feeling timely, I
went for the jugular. I asked if she could equate her eating disorder with her
mother's love. I quickly added, "It must be hard for you to resist these foods
since their loss seems to translate into having to nurture yourself both nutri-
tionally and emotionally." Linda was aghast but relented, "Truer words were
never spoken."

She then gave me a "gift" of a box of tissues and announced that when she
had used up the contents, therapy would be over. (Approach avoidance issues
seemed destined to surface.)

The next few months, Linda was continually depressed and resisted group
therapy. She continually struggled with her "secret" and vacillated about disclosure of her problems to Ted. She struggled with family of origin issues and
her "Madonna/whore syndrome." Her view of women as either "pure or
tainted" was connected to her Catholic upbringing and feelings about sex.
These beliefs were embedded in the doctrines of the Catholic Church as well
her notions about her mother. As a result, sex was defiled for her. The emphasis of the work revolved around intimacy with her husband and decreasing
her discomfort with sexual acts. Nevertheless, she still refused to involve Ted
in her treatment.

Ten months into therapy, Linda announced that she had finally confessed
to Ted: she had disclosed her eating disorder. Again, Ted requested to come
to treatment, but Linda resisted based on her fear that "If he found out the
awful truth, he would leave [her]." Interpretation of her fear of divorce led to
a frank conversation of her desire to self-sabotage and re-enact her mother's
role.

Linda declined, seemed discouraged, and admitted feeling powerless.
Unwilling to see me with Ted or have him see me separately, I asked her to
do a drawing of how she currently viewed herself. Linda depicted Figure 7-3,
a stick figure lying on the *tenth* line out of *nineteen* blue lines. *(Of interest was
the fact that she had been married **nineteen** years, her eating disorder had started
about **ten** years ago when her husband contracted melanoma and she had been molested at age **ten**.)* I pointed out that if she turned the picture vertically, she
appeared to be in jail.

Two sessions later (session 39), Linda told me that she felt it was time to ter-
minate therapy based on the following conclusions: her eating was under control, she had disclosed her "dark secret" to Ted (and he had remained
steadfast and supportive), and she felt better about herself. Instead, what she

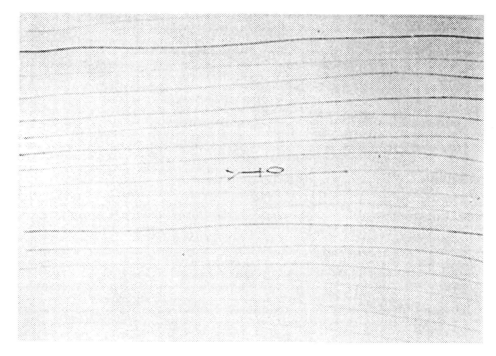

Figure 7-3. Linda's view of herself.

wanted to work on was her inability to speak publicly in front of others. Since she was quite intent on termination, I suggested that she continue in a stress-reduction therapy group at a local clinic and possibly see a colleague for biofeedback in continued psychotherapy. I felt that much work lay ahead for her and wondered if she would follow through with any of my recommendations. Somehow, in my heart, I knew that the obstacles were too difficult for Linda to hurdle. She had journeyed as far as she would allow herself to go during our year-long relationship. She had to close the door.

## THREE YEARS LATER

Linda called and tearfully begged me for an appointment. She revealed that when I heard "[her] story" that I might not want to minister her. She seemed quite desperate, so I arranged to see her the next day. Linda entered my office and tearfully informed me of several nodal events that had spanned the last three years: A few weeks prior, her brother-in-law, Bryant, had died of AIDS; her favorite aunt, Nancy, had contracted malignant cancer; and her son was angry with her because he had contracted viral Hepatitis B and could no longer drink with his cohorts. (This was the point in treatment that she chided herself for having "poisoned" her son with antibiotics prescribed to battle his constant earaches as a child.) I then linked her feelings of having been tainted by her mother's sugary treats to her belief that she had contaminated her son. She broke down and sobbed. It was then that she spilled the contents of "the story."

She apprised me of a psychiatrist who refused to treat her (based on her liabilities) and explained that she had attempted suicide by way of carbon monoxide poisoning. Currently, she was under the care of a physician who had prescribed Xanax™ for her depression. She admitted that her relationship with this doctor was "prescription therapy." I insisted that she see another psychiatrist if we resumed treatment. She accepted that proposition. I also affirmed the decision to include Ted in the next session. *Finally,* she agreed.

When Ted arrived, I pulled out the genogram (listed in the rear of this chapter) to discuss his perception of the family system and to focus on their marital relationship. The poison issue was raised and I interpreted her fantasy about killing her husband in our very first session and its reintroduction some 40 sessions later. Ted refuted Linda's hypothesis of defiling her son's health. He was genuinely concerned for her well-being and stated that he would comply with all of my suggestions.

Based on the issues at work, I recommended eventually incorporating Mitchell into treatment. Ted steadfastly refused, declaring, "He's coping pretty well." When I insisted that his presence would expedite treatment, he relented. Linda, however, was afraid to face Mitchell's wrath.

Linda arrived for our next individual appointment and we discussed the prior meeting with Ted. She doubted Ted's honesty and felt his attitude was saccharine. I asked her to project on the outside of a bag what he shares with her and what he sequesters inside the bag. The result is Figure 7-4. She represented Ted's "optimal" view of "life" and placed a picture of a man and a boy to illustrate the importance of his relationship with Mitchell. Shoes represented his need to work and interestingly enough they obliterated the man's face. She followed this descriptor by stating that Ted "threw himself into work" and then added that's why she had placed the words "money talks" on the bag. The words "eating poorly" and "Boca Raton" (their vacation plan) was covered up. On the other three sides and bottom of the bag was simply her name. She said that was how she experienced Ted and perceived herself: uni-dimensional, with Ted catering to her needs. Inside she placed a chocolate chip cookie affixed with the word "health." Apparently, Linda perceived Ted as also covering up his struggle with food issues.

Her next association was to her struggle with her faith. It was at this point that she emphasized that her marriage had never been blessed. She explained that post-marriage, she wanted to resolve this conflict. They both attended

Figure 7-4. Linda's view of Ted's take on life.

pre-cana workshops but never had their marriage blessed by the priest. I questioned why they had gone through the preparatory process and never completed this sacrament. She offered that they did not know two Catholics in good standing who would witness this event. After exploring this further, I learned that she was too embarrassed to go through this process despite the willingness of a couple with whom they occasionally socialized. I suggested that if it was discomfiture that was blocking her, that my (then) husband and I could witness this important event. She was shocked by both my offer and my conversion. I made light of the conversion, not delving into personal reasons and repeated my offer. She grappled for a response and an excuse. I suggested that she explore other possibilities with Ted since this obviously meant so much to her.

Somehow, I knew that she would never agree to my offer, but it was genuine and I raised the possibility for two reasons: (a) I felt that my conversion would serve as a springboard for exploring her nonrelationship with God (and it did) and (b) my disclosure served a dual purpose as both permission to explore the spiritual dimension in therapy and also as a catalyst for change.

At this time, the examination of Linda's spiritual dimension was merely a seed since family treatment took precedence. Several couple sessions followed. Linda relayed a story of mockingly calling Ted's secretary in Mitchell's presence and jokingly stating that both she and Mitchell "had no reason to go on." Mitchell became enraged and downed two beers in order to retaliate. Eventually, Ted and Linda agreed to bring Mitchell to a session. This was due in part to my interpreting a few points: (1) based on Linda's description of her enmeshed relationship with Mitchell and the "empty nest syndrome" that she was experiencing, I insinuated that perhaps Mitchell's illness offered him permission to come home again and (2) I implied that it might relieve Mitchell to know that his mother was indeed taking care of herself through therapy. However, I was duly warned not to bring up his illness. I consented and reiterated that I would respect the family's pace.

When they arrived, they reported only positive changes. Yet, Mitchell raised the issue of his illness without prompting from anyone. On his cue, I attempted to explore his depression and anger. He closed down and I reminded him that he raised the subject and perhaps he really did want to explore these issues. I invited him to come to the next meeting.

The next session was both a remarkable and moving session. Rather than working with art materials, I suggested that Mitchell use himself and his parents to construct a family sculpture. He structured himself between them in linear fashion yet referred to the shape as a triangle. I reflected its two-dimensional quality and recommended that he reconfigure the image three-dimensionally. He created an isosceles shaped triangle by having Linda lie at Ted and Mitchell's feet. Linda felt "protected" by her men. Again, I favored a change. This time, I asked Mitchell to construct the triangle how he idealized the situation. The shape was equilateral and all were holding hands. I interpreted his desire for such equality and pointed out its impossibility. As they sat down, Mitchell again brought up his illness. As before, he was resistant to discussing it and became sullen and angry. I touched him lightly on the arm and said that "on the contrary, I [thought] it would make [him] sad." Ted muttered, "Hmmm." Mitchell agreed. Linda sobbed and cried out "if only [she] could change things!"

I sat next to Mitchell and ***paradoxically*** suggested that perhaps he should comfort her. He did and she reflected that she felt her depression was due to

Mitchell's illness. Angry and not accepting this blame, Mitchell countered that he felt it was due to many factors. When I questioned what he meant, he mentioned Bryant's death, Linda's mother, Aunt Nancy, dead animals, and so the list went on.

I asked Mitchell to haul some empty chairs in the room and **symbolically position** them where they belonged. He was quite inventive in his seating arrangement of **twenty-six** empty chairs and thus he enabled his mother to view his illness in its proper perspective. This was double edged in relieving Mitchell's guilt within the context of his mother's illness. (Author's note: at one point when Mitchell kept adding empty chairs as stand-ins for people/animals or things that represented Linda's mourning and loss issues, I lightly joked about it. Mitchell remarked that his mother had lots of "issues" that clouded her recovery.)

It was clear at this juncture that some marital work was necessary in order to relieve Mitchell from his burden as caretaker. As well, Mitchell's obvious discomfort signaled Ted's need to be more responsive to his wife. About a month later, I met with Ted alone. He was depressed and felt guilt-ridden about rejecting Linda's depression and demanding that she "snap out" of her depression. I mirrored his need to place the onus on Linda and instead dismissed this as counterproductive. Moreover, I endorsed increased intimacy and supportive behavior as more comprehensive tools of expression. He agreed and decided to buy her flowers and take her on holiday for a few weeks.

Weekly sessions continued and Ted occasionally joined the sessions. Mostly, he prioritized his work and delegated Linda as the identified patient who needed treatment. Linda became increasingly depressed. I administered the Draw-A-Story test (Silver, 1992) and concluded that she be re-evaluated for a medication change. She agreed and after a few weeks, she was started on a minimum dosage of Prozac. Her affect seemed to improve with the drug and she was able to admit how lonely and isolated she felt from others. This confession helped me reintroduce her struggle with God and her need for community. After much deliberation around these issues and her apparent need for community (as outlined in Chapter 2 by Ashbrook (1971)), she introduced some changes–aerobics, horseback riding with Ted, and a commitment effort to reach out to others. She did not view herself as having friends and struggled with the concept of having one. She neither wanted a friendship with Ted nor with anyone else. Secretly, she longed for a friend whom she could turn off and on as easily as a "closet light bulb."

A few months later, Linda weaned herself off Prozac, was able to convince Mitchell to see a doctor about his condition, and had improved sexual relations with Ted.

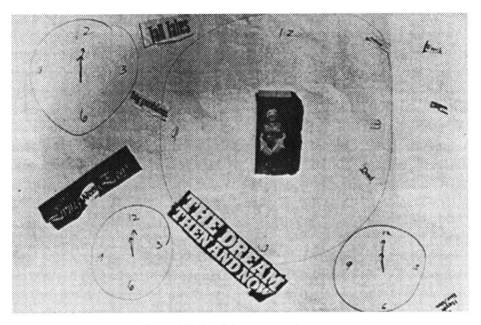

Figure 7-5. Linda's time running out.

Yet her depression resurfaced. Linda goaded Ted by arguing with him and accused him of "not loving" her because he hadn't asked, "what (she was) discussing with Ellen." Plus, Mitchell was making plans to move out and go back to school. This seemed more than she could handle. I suggested that she divide up a piece of paper into three areas designating her feelings about Ted, Mitchell, and herself. Oddly enough, she only focused on herself. Figure 7-5 is a collage of her feelings. She viewed the clocks as time running out.

The words had specific associations for her: Clockwise, "tall tales" referred to her stories and her projection that I disbelieved her; the small word, "jealousy" pertained to me and "anyone with a family" (Linda was quite annoyed that I had given birth since we first initiated therapy and had a chance to "do it right"); "wreck" simply implied how she felt about herself; "dead" corresponded to her ultimate ambition; "gothics" related to her pessimistic view of both the world and her personal situation; the upside-down positioning of "happily ever after" characterized her genuine hope as inverse; "the dream then and now" related to her "white picket fence" fantasy and the reality she now faced; the expression, "when the living was easy" again depicted her depression. Finally, the last words added, "the big problem" equated to her fear of Mitchell's illness and her projection that Ted would divorce her. The picture of the matronly grandmother was supposed to be self-representative.

It looked more like the dowdy portraits of her mother, suggesting identity conflicts, enmeshment, and boundary issues.

Thereafter, she spoke freely about her death wish. She viewed "death as a relief to (her) endless suffering." With that last comment, she announced that she and Ted were going on a two-week cruise. Although I felt the change of scene would be therapeutic, I worried about her suicidal ideation and prescribed a psychiatric consultation. Based on her verbal associates, previous suicidal ideation, and artwork produced, I was genuinely concerned for her safety.

For the next few months, Linda worked on her anger towards her mother (via creating voodoo dolls in therapy), and resolved Mitchell's move from home to a college campus. Many drawings revolved around this issue. Reinforcing her biofeedback therapy, I videotaped her in the privacy of my office. She was fragmented and obviously distraught. She erupted into tears, connected her mother to her low self-esteem, and chastised herself for neither getting her marriage blessed nor Mitchell baptized. This fostered her ability to acknowledge her contention with God and her spiritual arrestment.

Almost three years into treatment (for the *second* time), Linda finally had sufficient resolve to examine this constraint. She no longer hinted at the dichotomy nor avoided the "God topic." Instead, she prepared to do battle.


## THE SPIRITUAL WORK


Ironically, Linda's decision to undertake this journey preceded my month long vacation. In that last session, she had agreed to contact her friends, Louise and Peter, who previously agreed to witness the blessing of her marriage. Somehow, I suspected that she would procrastinate. So, being the obnoxious soul that I am, I sent her a congratulatory, wedding card while on vacation.

No surprise, she returned next with excuses about postponing the blessing. I insisted that she relinquish her shame and identification with her mother and proceed with her plans. She explained that part of her resistance was due in part to her fear that she might become "emotional" in Louise and Peter's presence and "break down" in front of them. This quandary was then equated to her incapacity to portray the "real, imperfect Linda." So, to force the point, I again offered myself as a witness. Here, she connected my proposal as a "pitiful reflection" of her weakness. *But I protested and compared my overture to the **same** concern I would have if she had an illness that required visitation at a hospital.* This was extremely important since correlating her spiritual arrestment to physical illness hit home. Since she was a medical doctor, somehow, I knew caging this in a clinical format would bypass her synapses of resistance. Again she agreed to call her pastor and set up a consultation. I urged her to discuss this with Ted by the following Monday *or* permit me to call him and apprise him of the situation. She agreed. By involving Ted (in this parental fashion), I hoped that Linda would rise to the occasion.

Monday rolled around and Linda hadn't called me. On Tuesday, I telephoned Ted. When Linda arrived next, I knew she harbored fantasies about the call, and so I addressed the subject. I suggested that she depict a drawing of what she thought I had revealed. A stick figure with a halo and cross above it was sketched next to the word hope. Under the word think, she placed a question mark. She feared that I had told Ted about her apprehension regarding her emotions, yet she stonewalled him and refused to discuss our telephone conversation. When I informed her that in fact I had discussed that problem, she was both aghast and relieved. I next suggested that she create wedding invitations and offer it to both Ted and Mitchell in order to facilitate a dialogue. Since she felt unable to present these in person, I offered to mail them for her. She agreed to that idea. However, she intercepted the mail and threw them away. I should have seen that coming and mailed it to Ted's office. Hindsight is 20-20.

The following meeting, Linda raised the subject of sexual abuse. She connected her adaptive behavior as a coping mechanism that no longer served its purpose. She likened this dissociation to her interlude from God and confirmed her desire to repair her relationship with Him. Indeed, she had called Jill and confessed her fears. While talking about Jill her jealousy surfaced because Jill's children were still at home. To streamline this discord, I asked her to construct a picture about her objectives in treatment. The rendering, titled "final frontier" (Figure 7-6) depicted a circle with a blackened wedge shape. She likened the wedge to her loneliness and "isolation from both God, family, and friends." Furthermore, she implied that she would never be "whole" until she overcame these obstacles. Little did she know how right she was.

Several months passed. We chipped away at these issues and one day she discussed the "demon in (her)." Intrigued by this metaphor, I then coaxed her into illustrating this conflict. To my surprise, she drew Maria and Cory without hands, surrounded them with fire, purposefully smashed charcoal on their faces, and then she renounced her demons (see Figure 7-7).

About a month passed. Linda continued to avoid contacting her priest. Finally, she called him and recounted a moving experience. She cried throughout their meeting and he asked her to call him for another appointment. When she failed to do so, he buttonholed her after church and she confessed her contention with forgiveness. As a result, I was able to associate her anger with God and her mother as synonymous and wondered aloud what it

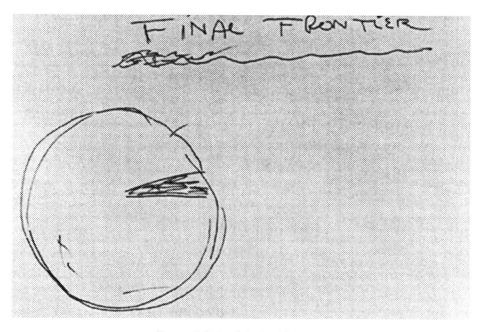

Figure 7-6. Linda's final frontier.

Figure 7-7. Linda's demons, Maria and Cory.

would mean for her to "forgive (herself) and get on with her life." I suggested that she listen to the words that the priest stated when he prepared himself for receipt of the sacraments:

> Through him, with him, in him. In the unity of the holy spirit, all honor and glory are yours forever and ever . . . Lord, Jesus Christ, you said to your apostles: I leave you peace, my peace I give to you. Look not on our sins, but on the faith of your church, and grant us peace and unity of your kingdom where you live forever and ever. Amen.

> This is the lamb of God who takes away the sins of the world. Happy are those who are called to his supper. Lord, I am not worthy to receive you but only say the words and I shall be healed. (*We Celebrate Missalette,* 1993, pp. 39–43.)

These words were not only unpalatable for Linda but also impossible for her to digest. She complained of forgiveness being "cheap." While her mother accepted the sacraments weekly, she was unable to sanction these gifts for herself. I focused on her need to condemn her mother and examined what it would be like for her to live in "gray land," as opposed to black and white. The result was Figure 7-8, a stark presentation of an axe with dripping blood. She explained that secretly she harbored fantasies about "axing (her) mother to death." But on the back she wrote the following words that represented the underlying depression connected to her anger: "lonely, sad, crying, smart, humor, eating, drinking, insomnia, fatigue."

A week later, I received a beautiful bouquet of flowers. Dumbfounded, I couldn't figure out who sent it or what it meant. The card read, "Thanks. The Newlyweds." After an hour or so, it dawned on me: Linda and Ted had their marriage blessed! I was thrilled for her and genuinely flabbergasted. (Years later, I still have that card. It serves as a reminder to remain true to this work I do that is based in spirituality.)

The following week, I learned more about why I received flowers. Naturally, I thanked her for the gift, and stated that perhaps I should be the one who sent them to her. Then, she disclosed that Ted almost missed the ceremony and had "meant to get (her) flowers but didn't find the time." I interpreted her need to send me the flowers she didn't get. She viewed the blessing of their marriage as simply "checking off" a list of self-induced requirements towards recovery. Still, she *refused* to forgive herself and *could not* partake in receiving the Eucharist.

Clearly, because of her religious upbringing, Linda needed to go to confession in order to atone for her sins and be forgiven. As Frank and Frank (1991) suggested, "confession is required for cure . . . impersonal forms of confession and repentance, as in some Christian liturgies, also serve the purpose of general purification" (p. 101).

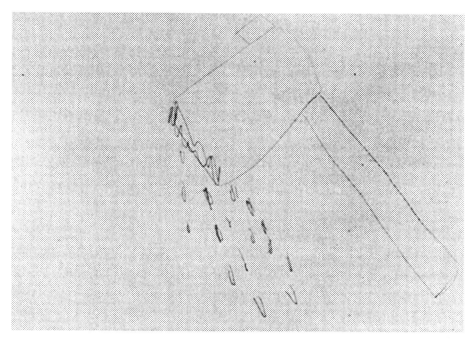

Figure 7-8. Linda's gray land–axing mother to death.

I was not surprised when her bingeing resurfaced. Linda blamed her mother and complained of her "control over (her)." I translated her mother's control as self-sabotage. Instead of hating her mother from afar, I suggested that she hate *me* for forcing her to do this work. The reason was twofold: (1) this encouraged a much needed dose of negative transference in order to progress and (2) simultaneously, it paved the pathway to forgiveness by recanting her hatred towards her mother and thereby permitting *forgiveness* from God.

Several months later, she had still made no headway. I suggested that she create a drawing, painting, or sculpture of what God meant to her (the first directive of the BATA). Figure 7-9 depicts Hell on one side, representing the devil, while the other side depicts "what God should mean to me," coupled by the words "confusing" and "emotional." A lightening bolt separated the positive and negative aspects of forgiveness. She then expressed her desire for God to "get angry at people, especially (her) mother." She echoed her confusion about the Catholic school doctrines and the contradictions she experienced. This led to a drawing of a blank circle, which she titled, "Bank of Linda." She clarified that when she raised Mitchell, his sycophantic presence simulated a "bank withdrawal." Yet the bank was empty. I connected her void to "no deposits from (her) own mother." She exploded into tears and her asso-

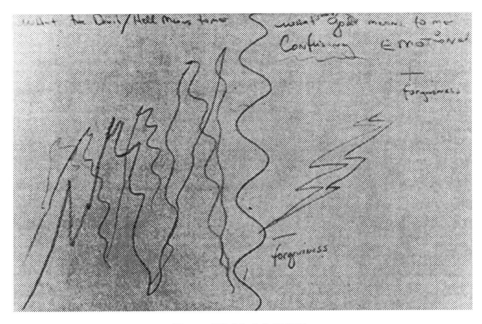

Figure 7-9. Linda's BATA.

ciation was of her mother "prancing around naked from the waist up" and how that contributed to her being so reserved with her own body and always "layering it and covering it up."

Verily, I was a tad surprised by her correlation and questioned what prompted her thinking. She then pointed to an unfinished canvas in the corner of my studio (Figure 7-10). The finished painting, which I have since titled "Heaven Scent," was the catalyst for this revelation!

Unlike Moon (1992), I *never* work on my own art when seeing a client. If I *join* a client in the art process, it is **always** related directly to the session work. Yet, from afar, my work instilled far-reaching proportions. Because this composition served to agitate a reactive state, I wondered about not only its impact but also its relevance to treatment. I pondered the positive and negative aspects of baring my art (no pun intended) and wrestled with whether or not to cover up future works in progress. Yet, this piece had a salutary effect on Linda's treatment. As a result of that incident, I no longer grapple with such notions. Although I am both responsible and accountable for the stimuli in my office, I have decided that my work need not be cloaked but, like other inducements, can serve as a useful tool for both verbal associates and inspiration. Thus, this artwork served as a springboard for Linda to recount this embarrassing tale. More importantly, however, it forged an avenue for Linda to connect her mother's overstimulating behavior directly to her prud-

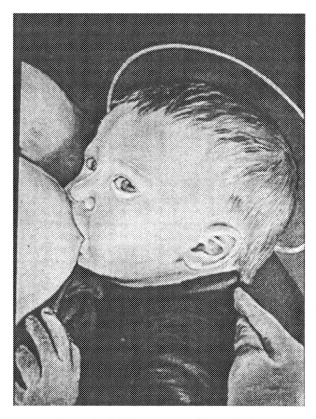

Figure 7-10. Heaven scent (by author).

ish, asexual demeanor. This aided my ability to penetrate these issues and encourage increased intimacy with Ted.

The next session, Linda wallowed in a sea of tears and resisted my attempts to comfort or care for her. Presumably, she had injured her foot during step aerobics and her physician had prescribed a course of physical therapy. She confessed that she had been going to aerobics class for approximately three hours per day, four days per week. During three different times in the session, she talked about "being up all night with God and a bottle" and thus alluded to a drinking problem. When I asked her to illustrate what she derived from this, she simply wrote "comfort." Again, I suggested that instead she envelop her family and faith community in her steadfast resolve to continue her SIB (self-injurious behavior). Unprepared for such intimacy, she rejected this notion and resolutely insisted her need to remain insular.

As well, my suggestion for inpatient hospitalization was met with similar disdain. When I called her psychiatrist, he thanked me and said he would "assess" the situation in their next meeting. Nevertheless I was concerned since her next appointment with him was not for another three weeks.

Later that week, Linda telephoned me and revealed that her supervisor and coworker had walked into Ted's office and announced that they had made an appointment for her at the local mental health center because of her "anorexia" and recent physical problems with walking. I told her that this might have been a blessing in disguise. She was both annoyed and grateful for their intrusive behavior. I suggested her need to welcome their concern. She agreed and actually expressed relief.

Over the next month, Linda was referred to a pain clinic to help diagnose this physical ailment which had suddenly developed. Finally, her physical problem was given a name—Reflex Sympathetic Dystrophy Disorder (RSDD). (Apparently, Linda's RSDD was the combination of psychological stressors, injury from step aerobics, and an eating disorder that exacerbated her condition. The disease *itself* is usually related to some type of injury coupled with a psychological predisposition that sustains the nerves and synapses to continually send pain messages to the brain.) Nevertheless this nebulous condition is an esoteric and debatable diagnosis. I contacted the local Muscular Dystrophy Association in order to learn more about a local or national chapter of RSDD.

Evidently, the only form of treatment was a limited course of spinal pain blocks that could foster recovery or partial relief. If the pain became unbearable, the alternative was either a chemical or surgical sympathectomy—elective paralysis to cut off the pain. Naturally, that was not a consideration for Linda. She elected to begin a course of spinal blocks and receive a daily regiment of Elavil™ (125 mgs at bedtime) to counter her knee swelling and offer some relief. (Oddly enough, Elavil™ is also the drug of choice for anorexia and depression. So, this served a dual purpose. It also aided Linda's insomnia and substituted her need to rely on "God and a bottle.")

Strangely enough, Linda suddenly confessed her fear that she "might never see (me) again and how much (she would) miss me." After some prodding, I learned that her fear of abandonment was directly linked to Ted. He professed little sympathy for his wife's condition and voiced disdain when she wallowed in self-pity. Instead, he refused to discuss the situation and suggested that Linda maintain a positive outlook in order to expedite recovery. Yet Linda needed both his impartial understanding and his support. He refused her either. Moreover, although her "colleagues" initially offered support by way of flowers and visitation, the contacts waned. She felt truly alone in her battle. As her only option, she feared that I, too, would forsake her. Again, I interpreted the simile to God.

After her initial pain block, Linda walked to the end of her street. By my insistence via a weekly chart, her eating also appeared markedly improved:

she was eating three, sensible meals per day. Yet, she was resistant to the notion of improved health. The eternal pessimist, Linda was unwilling to perceive herself as better. Instead, it was easier to remain sick.

After several weeks and another pain block, Linda was much improved. She was able to walk for about an hour. Yet, her attitude was grim and depressed. Unable to work, she resigned herself to remaining on disability and quit her job. Since her vocation offered Linda the only means for social contact, sacrificing this position was quite a dichotomy. She openly admitted that she prayed nightly for death. Nevertheless, she insisted that she was not suicidal and discounted such action due to how it would impact Mitchell. She whined repeatedly about "not wanting to cope anymore."

My countertransference set in. I felt both sorry for her and simultaneously annoyed and angry. It infuriated me that she positively resisted wellness and refused to recognize her gains. I knew that my response hinged on her suicidal, depressive mode. Even my process notes smacked of statements such as, "I think I am slipping into the hate-patient mode."

Troubled by my countertransference, I sought supervision from a colleague and friend. Over lunch, we were able to exchange parables of depressed, suicidal patients and laughed about their power to cause so much duress.

Later, my colleague helped normalize my feelings by sharing an article with me. Psychiatrists Maltsberger and Buie (1974) warned that the therapist's repression, reaction formation, projection, and denial of countertransference hatred increased the danger of suicide. They also reported that countertransference is "likely to be particularly intense in the treatment of 'borderline' and psychotic patients, especially those who are prone to suicide" (p. 625).

In fact, the aversive impulse tempts the therapist to abandon the patient. Moreover, Maltsberger and Buie discovered that suicidal patients tend to "evoke the sadism of others" but later summarized that while a sadomasochistic relationship is both undesirable and destructive, "it is better than no relationship at all" (p. 626). They concluded that the best protection from "antitherapeutic acting out" is the ability to keep impulses in the realm of consciousness. Indeed, a more complete defense incorporates the therapist's comfort with his countertransference hate via acknowledgement and perspective:

> When the onslaught of the transference is met not with narcissistic overweaning and regressive acting out, when the therapist can maintain the relationship in an appropriately interested way, the patient has a chance to acknowledge his transference for what it is, to learn to bear the intensity of his craving and rage, and put them into perspective. The patient may exchange his impossible narcissistic dreams for real relationships once he finds their fulfillment is not necessary for his survival. (Maltsberger & Buie, 1974, p. 632)

Although the aforementioned advice coupled with peer supervision enabled me to overcome my countertransference hate battle, this work exacted much composure on my part. Linda's lack of improvement grated on my narcissistic need to be the effective and competent therapist that I imagined myself to be. It became increasingly difficult to tolerate Linda's regression and hatred.

Insult added to injury as Linda's bingeing resurfaced. I inquired how she felt about being weighed. (Although this is counter to some of the literature on anorexia, I felt that this might actually enhance her treatment.) She agreed to the idea only if the weight was not revealed. I settled on a weekly recording of her weight and promised not to disclose the results.

On the first weigh in, at 5'8", she came in at 120 pounds. Considering that she was fully clothed and wearing lightweight boots, my guess was that her actual weight would have been more like 116 pounds. Although this did not seem disastrous, I was astonished at how little she framed. Two weeks later, she weighed in at 125 pounds. Linda continually referred to herself as "trapped" by her body, so I directed her to illustrate how that felt. The result, Figure 7-11, was a tiny stick person, disconnected at the body and groin, devoid of arms. Both legs were caught in traps labeled "Corey" and "Maria." At the base of each trap lies an axe. Because of the obvious castration anxiety and fear of bodily harm connected to her association of Maria and Corey's "hold" over her, I asked her to delineate how it felt when she "was out of her trapped body."

Her drawing response was not at all surprising. Linda drawing suggested a desire to dissociate from her current condition. She blamed everything on Maria and Corey. I disagreed and insisted that it was she who was in charge of her traps and creating her own pain. "Maybe," she meekly responded. I further insinuated that she had the power to free herself from the pain, yet perhaps she achieved some secondary gain from the trap. She agreed. Moreover, I suggested that she had not truly expressed her feelings through the art and that perhaps we work with a more resistant material, such as clay or wood.

The next week, she created a clay image of her mother, stabbed her in the crotch, and then proceeded to give her a lobotomy with a needle tool. Linda seemed to derive much satisfaction from this work (Figure 7-12).

The following week, I offered Linda wood and she seemed comforted by its ability to withstand her anger. She expressed the "venom" which she had harbored for years as akin to "swallowing a rattler." As she continued to hack away, she verbalized hatred towards her mother. She pounded, hammered, and chiseled and voiced, "I just want to smash her face with my fist!" When I suggested that her hatred was also connected to her lost childhood and parental deprivation, she ended the session and stated, "It's time to go."

Figure 7-11. Linda trapped by her body.

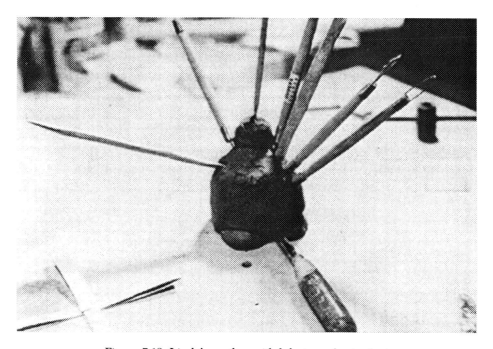

Figure 7-12. Linda's mother with lobotomy/castration.

I relented, but before she took her leave, she mentioned forgiveness and her contention that she would never go to Heaven. I implied that some people believed that if people prayed for a soul that one would ascend to Heaven anyway. I also suggested her need to resolve her differences with her mother (in this life) if she were planning a "peaceful hereafter." This was a formidable pill for her to swallow so I dropped the discussion and let her mull over the possibilities.

A few weeks later, the discussion again focused on forgiveness. I asked her to write a list of her sins that precluded forgiveness from God. She listed: (1) no religion for Mitch, (2) abusive mother, (3) hate—Maria and Corey, and (4) forgiveness. In elaborating, Linda remarked that she couldn't "buy into" the principle of forgiveness and that this had overtaken her relationship with God. Unlike the Christian proverb, she could not "turn the other cheek" (as suggested by Jesus regarding accepting the ill-mannered behavior of others). Yet in ignoring this maxim, her self-hatred was so grave that she had simultaneously turned away from her God. She repeated the story of a nun's warning that divorce always resulted in Hell. In defense of her mother, whom she both loved and hated, she felt forced to turn her back on this unjust God in order to remain loyal and steadfast to her mother. What a dilemma! The only way she could truly resolve this conflict was to return to the church, confess her sins, and *accept* God's forgiveness.

The following week, I pulled out her list of sins and suggested that she burn them in order to symbolize her need to release her soul from this self-imposed burden. We watched it burn in silence. She then confessed that en route to therapy, she had prayed for her mother's death. She also admitted praying more frequently and was able to state that on some level, she had forgiven her mother and no longer blamed her for her entire life situation. She also was able to accept that she must have been a better mother than she had thought since she actually had a very good relationship with Mitchell. We discussed Ted's responsibility for not insisting that Mitchell be baptized and I highlighted his agnostic stance and her subservient need to "follow his lead." More importantly, I underscored that it was no longer her responsibility to baptize Mitch. I then stated that even though she couldn't forgive herself for her "sins," perhaps God already had.

She seemed perplexed so I told her the New Testament story of Zacchaeus, who collected taxes from the people and pocketed most of the money. When Jesus had come to town, a great crowd gathered to see Him. Zacchaeus, small in stature, could not see above the crowd and so he climbed a nearby sycamore tree. When Jesus saw Zacchaeus, he exclaimed, "Come down from there. I am going to your house to have dinner with you." The town's people were shocked that Jesus would socialize with such an evil man. But when Zacchaeus had returned the next day, Jesus had pardoned his sins and Zacchaeus had repented and vowed to repay the money he owed to all the people. The moral behind this story was that people *could* change, repent, and be forgiven. This parable paved the road toward forgiveness and exploration of Linda's arrested spiritual dimension.

The following week, Linda was distressed about turning 50 and being simultaneously jobless and disabled. I implied that it might help her to again work with the wood. As she chipped away, I mentioned an article that I had read in the RSDD newsletter: it stated that many people subscribed to the notion of prayer and faith as a curative factor in RSDD. Linda coldly stated, "It works for some people." Then, she began to cry and asked if she could "leave early" in order to "get control" over her feelings. Although I urged her stay, she refused. As I later wrote up the session, I realized that Linda had fallen apart when the discussion turned to prayer and faith.

When Linda arrived the following week, I lifted up a napkin to reveal a carrot cake, which I had baked for her birthday. We lit the candles and she made a wish. Although she was hesitant to eat with me and/or in front of me, I persuaded her to join me in this celebration. While eating, I inquired about her need to leave during the last session. She could not recall what prompted this reaction. I reminded her of our discussion about the RSDD newsletter and the preponderance of faith and prayer as a prescription for pain. I speculated about her desire to be responsible for her own healing (via faith).

A few weeks later, Linda announced that she felt an overall improvement. Yet this was stained by her skepticism that this respite would be short-lived. I gingerly interpreted her pessimism and concomitant need to remain "sick." Rather, I proposed that perhaps the panacea would be for her to truly adopt the social mask she adorned since it was truly self-serving. Surprised by my **paradoxical** directive, I pressed her further. I insisted that she don this guise via her art. She created Figure 7-13, a smiling sun and a tiny figure, cut in half at the waist, atop of a falling ladder. The title "what it would be like to actually be positive" belies the feeling.

She expressed her fear of reaching toward the sun and falling off the ladder. I asked her to then close her eyes and imagine a color connected to the pinnacle of health. She saw yellow. This cleared a pathway for discussion. I broached the concept of the sixth dimension as outlined by Hettler (1979). Perplexed, Linda inquired about how she could develop her spiritual dimension. We discussed her desire and need to have faith in herself and God.

I beseeched her to believe in herself and rekindle her childhood hope. Tears began to fall. Her leg shook under the table. "How can I do that?" she insisted. I suggested that perhaps she could start by accepting herself and stop trying to be the "smartest, thinnest, hardest worker." More tears. I then handed her a reading from the *We Celebrate Missalette* (1993) and asked her to read it and then illustrate it. It reads:

Figure 7-13. Linda's view of being positive.

A reading from the letter of Paul to the Romans.

We know that all creation groans and is agony even until now. Not only that, but we ourselves, although we have the Spirit as first fruits, groan inwardly while we await the redemption of our bodies. In hope we were saved. But hope is not hope if its object is seen; how is it possible for one to hope for what he sees? And hoping for what he cannot see means awaiting it with patient endurance.

The spirit too helps us in our weakness, for we do not know how to pray as we ought; but the Spirit himself makes intercession for us with groanings, which cannot be expressed in speech. He who searches hearts know what the Spirit means, for the Spirit intercedes for the saints as God himself wills. The Word of the Lord. (Romans 8/22-27)

Figure 7-14 pictures a stick-like representation with tears flowing from "X'ed" out eyes. The crossed eyes appear to reject both internal and external stimuli. The figure is crushed beneath a misshapen world, which teeters off course. A cloud of "hope" floats aimlessly above the world. Despondent, she expressed a desire to leave early. I let her go but not before I interpreted her aversion to any discussion, which embraced spiritual development or God. I suggested that perhaps when she left, she continue to pray—perhaps to go to church or simply commune with God, *anywhere.* Confounded, she left; I believe she heard me.

In discussing prayer, Price suggested that it is indeed fellowship. He stated:

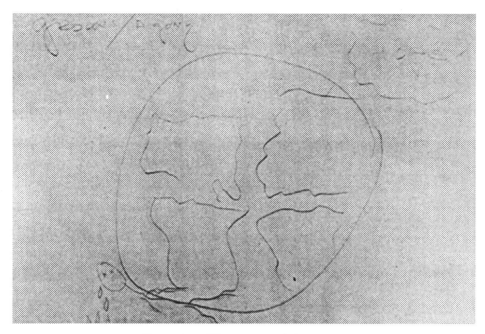

Figure 7-14. The groan and the agony.

In prayer, we not only contemplate God; we speak to Him and He answers us. Prayer is not only communion, but renewal. We come to God in our weakness to be made strong; in our ignorance to be made wise; in our sickness to be made well; in our sorrow to be made happy; in our sin to be made righteous; and what we need we receive, if only we come in the right spirit and dare to believe that we may have the thing for which we ask. (1983, p. 16)

Several weeks later, Linda had improved significantly. She had revamped her curriculum vitae, started swimming lessons, and sent Mitchell an article on rites in Christian adulthood penned by Ann Landers. She then showed me her church bulletin, which announced a new group for "all those who suffer." When I asked if she were planning to join, she mockingly rebuffed the idea. So I asked her to do a drawing about what faith meant to her. The result is Figure 7-15. The crying tadpole figure (perhaps still evolving) bears the weight of a cross. I inquired as to whether or not she could do a drawing of faith without relying on religion. She couldn't. For Linda, there was no separation. Faith and God were intrinsically joined.

Linda's ability to accept her physical wellness waxed and waned. Instead, she constantly reminded her body of her illness until she induced a slight setback. I wondered how much was real and how much was merely self-induced. I suspected the latter. Many times she compared herself to Sisyphus, the mythological character beset with the challenge of constantly pushing a

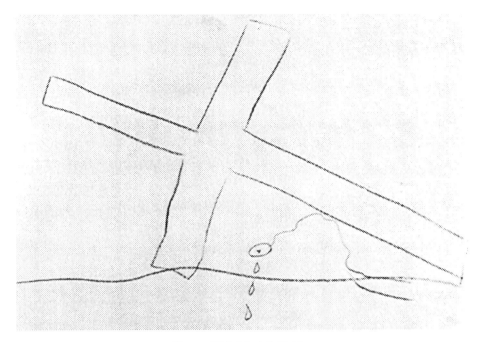

Figure 7-15. Linda's Faith.

boulder uphill. Repeatedly, she drew figures crushed by the rock and whined about her inability to continue to cope. Even though, I pointed out her gains, she wallowed in self-pity. Nevertheless, she forged ahead and continued to search for employment.

The next week she interviewed at Planned Parenthood and wrestled with a multitude of factors. Even though she desperately wanted the job, she struggled with her ardent Catholicism and stance on abortion. Always, she had thought of herself as politically "pro-choice." However, she was now faced with the possibility of crossing picket lines and assuaging her guilt by telling herself that she was helping women get proper medical treatment. She was unsure if she would take the job even if it were offered. I voiced the idea of creating a list outlining the pros and cons of the job. The pros outweighed the cons. Actually, she believed it to be a moot point; she was convinced that she would not be offered the job.

In an article on the nature of work, Chittister (1993) posed the following question: is work a punishment for sin or an opportunity for spiritual growth? A recent survey at the Center for Ethics and Corporate Policy reported that most Americans believed their work to be very important to their spirituality. Scripture, too, is quite clear about the place of work. The Book of Genesis instructs us to till the garden of life and keep it. We are expected to take care of what we have been given Yet, sin makes what we are meant to do more difficult. Linda struggled with this sense of sin and wrestled with how closely she could work with birth control and abortion and be exempt from sin. And Genesis is quite explicit: we work to complete the work of God in this world.

According to Chittister, there are two negative poles of work:

> one pole is workaholism, the other is pseudo-contemplation. The workaholic uses work as a substitute for other things in life. . . .Work can be what guards us from having to make conversation. . . . Workaholics can become their work. If it is valued, they are valued. (1993, p. 6)

Linda fit this description aptly. For her, when work was over, her very reason for existence was over. She defined herself through her work. This sad distortion of God's will for human work implied a tragic end to an exciting possibility. (But honestly, I could relate.)

In discussing pseudo-contemplation, Chittister states: that "holy leisure is not a license to live irresponsibly." She goes on to state, "Co-creation is a mandate written deep in the human heart. Work itself is holy" (1993, p. 6). She aptly purports work's relation to community and its ability to enrich the social fabric of humanity. And with Linda, her contributions in fact improved community and gave her a sense of purpose and well-being. Was that really so bad?

A week later, I received a joyful message on my voicemail at work and my answering machine at home: Linda had landed the job. When I congratulated her, she cancelled our next appointment since it conflicted with her new schedule. I accommodated my appointment book to set up a new time. When she arrived, she bubbled over with elation. Still, she continually questioned her work as sin. She ended the session by suggesting that we see each other every two weeks. I reminded her that the last time we had set up that precedent, her friends made an appointment for her at the local mental health clinic. Aghast, she pooh-poohed the notion of a relapse. Nevertheless, I agreed with her request. Before she left, again she raised doubts about her job. I stated that perhaps this was not a "test" as she had implied, but a blessing. According to Prasinos:

> One can view events in the client's life as part of God's curriculum. One can have hope in the most difficult case. One can feel spiritually united with a healing force that extends our helplessness far beyond what we would be capable of alone. (1992, p. 48)

In the words of Chittister, "Work is our gift to the future. It is our sign that God goes on working in the world through us. It is the very stuff of divine ambition . . . God needs us to complete God's work. Now" (1993, p. 9).

Linda will probably perpetuate a life-long struggle with God. Until, she quiets that inner voice, accepts herself, and forgives herself and God, her spiritual dimension will indeed suffer. At least now, both she and I are equipped with the accouterment to settle this ongoing argument. The warring with God seems to be temporarily suspended. Like the 1993 Arab/Israeli peace accord, there seems to be an agreement, a treaty to halt this infraction. Like the neighboring Israelites and Palestinians, I can't help wondering how long, this accord?

Finally, this work that I do is an exercise in love. It is arduous, difficult, trying, perplexing, and every once in a while, it is truly rewarding. Work is truly its own asceticism. What work yields is our dues, our tilling, our way of perpetuating God's gift. If we do it well, then spirituality will abound. And we ***need not*** even mention ***God, love or spirit.*** Truly, preaching and dogmatism run counter to the acceptance so fundamental to this work of therapy. Yet by operating in this spiritual paradigm, both client and therapist develop the capacity for the unitive. Spirituality has always been woven into the fabric of psychotherapy. It is a sacred, holy ceremony founded on interpersonal communion. The work is never over. As Tolstoy once wrote, "The sole purpose of life is to serve humanity."

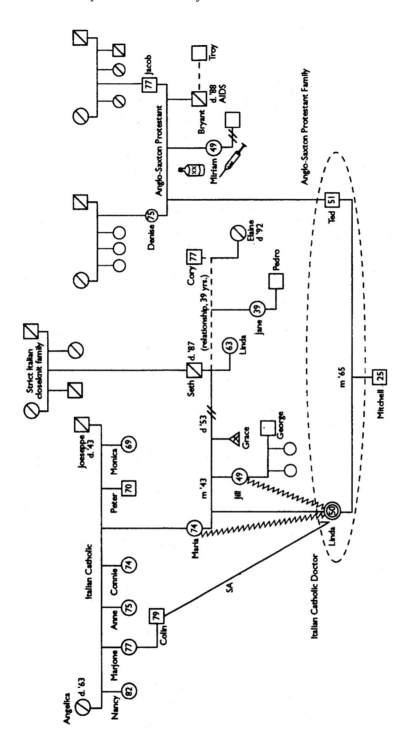

Genograms and Timeline of Linda

Genograms and Timeline of Linda (Continued)

INDA

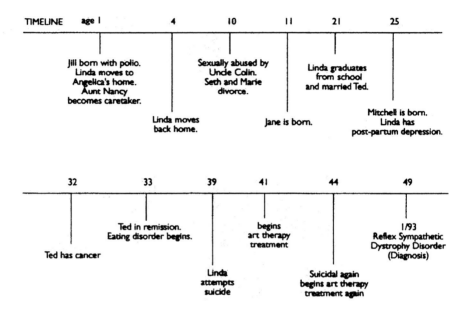

TIMELINE    age 1        4        10        11        21        25

Jill born with polio. Linda moves to Angelica's home. Aunt Nancy becomes caretaker.

Linda moves back home.

Sexually abused by Uncle Colin. Seth and Marie divorce.

Jane is born.

Linda graduates from school and married Ted.

Mitchell is born. Linda has post-partum depression.

32        33        39        41        44        49

Ted has cancer

Ted in remission. Eating disorder begins.

Linda attempts suicide

begins art therapy treatment

Suicidal again begins art therapy treatment again

1/93 Reflex Sympathetic Dystrophy Disorder (Diagnosis)

# Chapter 8

# SPIRITUAL REFRAME:
# A PATHWAY FOR LIFE

*Think of yourself as an incandescent power,*
*illuminated perhaps and forever talked to by God and His messengers.*

*—Brenda Ueland*

In the Old Testament, Moses ascends Mount Sinai and returns a changed man. His wife, shocked by his appearance, realizes that he has witnessed God. It is apparent both in the expression he dons and the task he claims to bear. In describing his experience, Moses reveals God's truth and attests that, "His spirit is in all of us."

Thousands of years later, many are claiming this same truth (see Eadie, 1992). Either we haven't progressed very far or humankind has been unreceptive to listening. Whatever the reason, as Halpern stated in the Foreword of this book: "To read meaning into existential events and landmarks, whether spawned by religious doctrine, piety, folklore, or superstition, remains at the very heart of the human struggle to fathom the seemingly impenetrable essence of man's relationship to creation and the Creator" (p. viii).

And so, we perpetuate that struggle in our everyday existence. Just as human beings are guided by physiologic and psychologic principles that we cannot begin to comprehend or challenge, our collective unconscious is also guided by such unknown controls. Handed down from our ancestors, seasoned by genetic coding, humanity continually grapples with this incessant search for meaning. It is our destiny. Curious animals that we are, we ceaselessly examine our reason for existence. Constantly, we search for a "greater purpose," something at least that offers import.

Admittedly, if humankind accepts the tenets of Moses and sanctions this message, perhaps the struggle will be over. Like Ueland suggests above, this would require that we bear our cross, embrace our utter connectedness to this Higher Power, and conspire with the Will of God by allowing His spirit to become our own. A seemingly simple task mired in the existence of two highly-charged details: belief and faith. Perhaps since mankind contends so ardently with both belief and faith systems, we might never transcend this struggle and sojourn into the arms of contentment, ultimate satisfaction, and unconditional nurturance.

Clearly, these highly-desired aspirations are within our reach. Yet, as much as human beings claim to truly want this end, we contend, and contend, and contend. But why? Why not simply give in to the mystery? Why not be sated? Why not be blissful? Is it humankind's ultimate neurosis? Is it the Woody Allen persona of the spiritual world to continuously head off this advance? Is it a reflection of humankind's perpetual need to struggle? Perhaps. Although human beings routinely claim their desire for transcendence, when it comes right down to it, maybe they really prefer to suffer and be miserable. For we are an odd lot. It seems when we are faced with peace, ultimately, we choose war.

And so resolutely, we reject faith. Instead, we hinge our souls on resistance, despair, wretchedness, venom, and turmoil. As hedonistic as civilization has become, people invariably reject the quintessential indulgence of spirit and soul. We look in all the wrong places, instead of seeking succor from within.

## THE ULTIMATE TABOO

Sweet (1990), in discussing the characteristics of shamanistic writing, brutally writes about creativity in such a forthright and honest manner that sunglasses are almost prerequisite. Like Freud, Sweet declares that the "greatest tension comes from the expression of a taboo" (p.22). He suggests that in unearthing what one needs to most write about, that the author:

> . . . make a list of cultural taboos, find one that personally makes you sweat the most–ones that you've repeatedly dreamed about night and day–and then assume yourself sufficiently energized to explore that tension. Writing, after all, is a form of ripping, exposing, revealing, of exorcising what one's particular society and what one's particular self has trouble forbidding. (Sweet, 1990, p. 21)

I hope I have done that. The subject matter of spirituality breeds one of two possible positions: unconditional relief and acceptance or incredible discomfort. I knew that when I began this treatise. I knew the topic alone would serve to both envelop some while rejecting others. The idea of adopting a spiritual reframe in psychotherapy is clearly not a gray issue. Either one welcomes this tenet or renounces it. There is nothing in between about it. But, then again, accepting one's own spirituality is not exactly a colorless consequence. Au Contraire! Instead, the spectrum is neither black nor white: alas, it is primary, secondary, and tertiary all at once.

Others have also sojourned down this hallway. In preparing for the 24th Annual American Art Therapy Conference, Cathy Moon sent out a questionnaire inquiring about whether or not there was an inherent relationship between spirituality and making art. Varied were the responses, which she received. Yet at the opening session in her topic, *Mystery: The Guiding Light,* Cathy concluded the following:

> The beneficent spiritual art therapist would remain firmly grounded in the reality of the tangible world while acknowledging the intangible, ineffable aspects of life. In practice, the making of art would provide such a grounding for therapist and patient alike. (1994, p. 21)

She further delineates the role of the art therapist as assisting the client via exploration, identification, and expression of personal belief systems. This allows for viewing spirituality as inherently human, not foreign.

Accepting this pathway requires that the clinician embrace an authentic, empathic position while gently guiding the learner/patient toward recovery. And it matters not if the zone abuts the walkways of "faith" or "God." The therapist, per force, is obligated to be open, flexible, and *congruent* with that person's value or faith system.

Sweet also flirted with this concept in discussing his view of shamanistic writing, a theosophy that incorporates the use of soul, coupled with art. He aptly wrote:

> Pens and paint and clay and musical notes are not safe toys for rigid adults. Only children are guileless enough to use them naturally and well. In this area– and perhaps this area alone–the child is indeed father to the man. . . . Sight, smell, hearing, and feeling are accumulations of our entire lives. Memory is who we are. (1992, p. 11)

And what we are. After all, both our patients' realities and our own are based on memory. Nothing more and nothing less. The trick in acclimating toward wellness is the way in which we use our memory. Indeed, here we must also include the memory of our collective unconscious. We *cannot* ignore this. For if we dare, it will raise its ugly little head again and again and again until we accept our archetypes, swallow them whole, and above all, *trust* them. Verily, it is in the digestion that the ascension either flourishes or withers. Alas, we can choose to spit them out, regurgitate their lesson, or absorb their instruction and come up whole. What a concept! Digestion and holistic medicine all rolled into one framework. Or perhaps it could be better called, we are what we eat.

However one describes it, the bottom line is that we become what we can. We open ourselves up to this mystery **when** we are able. It is **only** then that we truly can reframe ourselves and our clients in this image.

Here's to your memory. May you prosper and grow.

# Chapter 9

# PHOTOTHERAPY APPLICATIONS:
# EXPLORING MOURNING AND LOSS ISSUES

Mit vos far an oigmen kult oif ainem, aza ponem hot er–
The way you kook at a man, so he appears to you

*—Dictionary of Popular Yiddish Words, Phrases and Proverbs*

## MOURNING AND LOSS ISSUES: FINDING ONE'S
## BELIEFS THROUGH IMAGES

According to Fowler's (1981) belief system, cultural and mythical stories handed down from generation to generation inform our biology and make us who we are in the world. Yet another way in which humankind has chronicled stories has been through visual imagery. Years before daguerreotypes were invented, portraiture via painting and sculpture was the manner in which familial history was passed down. With the advent of photographic imagery, visual keepsakes became available for the common person. While portraiture is still readily available and used, photographic images offer a different avenue into the human psyche when exploring familial and /or unresolved conflicts.

While there are numerous mechanisms for exploring mourning and loss issues, one of the easiest routes is utilizing personal snapshots. When photographic albums are brought to the treatment table, working with these images can facilitate recovery in myriad ways: Phototherapy can encompass academic and or clinical exploration from the following perspective: studio investigation, self and group inquiry, Polaroid transfer and emulsion photocopy transfer, cyanotype printing, digital photography, videography, and Luminous emulsions on paper, wood, metal, and ceramic. Art responses created by my past graduate students enrolled in a Phototherapy class will highlight the efficacy of the aforementioned techniques and underscore the inherent possibilities of these functions from both academic and clinical perspectives. As well, three brief clinical vignettes that follow will illustrate some of the ways in which Phototherapy techniques can be utilized with myriad patient populations.

## ACADEMIC APPLICATIONS

In the mid 1990s, when pursing my doctoral degree, I enrolled in a five-day poetry workshop led by the eminent Dr. Carol Barrett. Conducted at the UCLA campus, this was an opportunity to retreat into the poetic ministries of the written word. While going through this training, one of the exercises chosen by Dr. Barrett was to hand out two or three index cards, each containing one random line of text from myriad resources (journals, newspapers, magazines). From these cards, we were instructed to create a poem in less than 10 minutes. The poem, which I penned, became one of the most telling dips into phototherapy that I had ever written: The words I arbitrarily received were "I used to come here as a child" and "But what of the things we left." This verse contained hidden clues as to how I made sense of my childhood by combing over pictures of my youth and family:

The Mahogany Drawer

I used to come here as a child—
that long, dank narrow space,
looming inside my mind.
I sorted through pictures of your memory,
the only thing worth preserving that I kept.

I used to come here as a child—
that mahogany, bottom drawer,
replete with glossy photos, embedded
with your history.

I used to come here as a child—
and pretend that your black and
white existence would lend glossy
texture to my tattered and broken heart.

I used to come here as a child—
and sift through the sea of photographs
that lined the walnut-stained images
of my sepia-toned hues of your color.

I used to come here as a child—

and bury myself in the comfort of your memory,
more real than any
that you left me.

Yes, I used to come here as a child–
always hoping, praying, to find you
real in those long-ago places,
now buried in your institutionalized,
and vapid mind.

I used to come here as a child–
but no longer do I visit that ebony rimmed,
mahogany container that was you.

But what of the things we left?

After I wrote this poem, I was stunned by its evocative nature and what it unleashed in my core. This truly concretized how photographic images reveal our history and our biology. Later, I expanded on that theory in my second text (Horovitz, 1999).

Soon after that workshop, I found myself teaching my first phototherapy class. New to this particular venue, I scoured the research and read the more historical texts of Krauss and Fryear (1983) and Fryear and Corbit (1992). But truly, it wasn't until I read the work of Weiser (1993) that I really understood the phototherapy in which I had been operating. The beauty of phototherapy, which can be understood as a variety of ideologies, which examine pictures of one's past to creating pictures/photographs/sculptures/videos, et cetera from one's current perspective, is that the inherent work has the "ability to immediately trigger memories, trigger affect, put the client back into that feeling state" (Krauss, 1979) in a way that actually no other medium can. As an art therapy clinician, I have patients with complex etiologies such as Asperger's syndrome, autism, and aphasia of varying typology. Indeed, I have repeatedly witnessed the power of photographic images in accelerating recovery in these often unreachable patients. But from a historical viewpoint, it is indeed understandable. As Weiser suggests:

> We can only be aware of ourselves to the extent that we can self-reflect; our existence at any moment is a summary of selective memory and, within the distortive nature of that process, also a partial fiction created only by what we can know of ourselves and have introjected from others. (1993, p. 20)

This is especially true when working with people who have temporarily lost their memory (for example through traumatic brain injury) as well as those who are enduring the cruel reality of the varying stages of Alzheimer's and dementia. Not being able to recall one's history is a callous existence that impacts not only the individual suffering from this altered state but that person's loved ones. Truly, phototherapy can be used for almost any kind of affliction. It is especially useful when working on death-related trauma and loss. I have been incorporating familial photographs of clients to advance mourning and loss issues for over 20 years and truly the evocative power of a photograph can kick through the most hardened defenses and veneers. It can be used as the medium of choice or even a jolt for digging into deeper recesses towards wellness and recovery.

The old maxim "a picture is worth a thousand words" truly has meaning when working with non-verbal clients. Photographs coupled with music can also stimulate untold emotive responses. Just look to the power behind a musical score coupled with a photographic scene in a movie. Paired with just the right music, even a deftly woven, 30-second, commercial advertisement broadcast on television can reduce the masses into mush.

Perhaps the reason behind such powerful craft lies in the archetypes, which we assign to these images. For whatever reason, photographic images have been used throughout time to affect the masses from psychology (the Thematic Apperception Test–a projective test where one makes up a story about each photographic image which is presented) to current day cinematography. The image is and always will be a most powerful and therapeutic avenue for exploring emotions. Looking at a photographic image, one goes back in time to that exact spot and perspective where the image was taken. Little else can move a person so close to recovering memory.

## STUDENT SAMPLES

In my phototherapy class, I use a variety of techniques to shake up a student's perspective on the uses of this powerful, medicinal uptake and its application when working with various clients.

The phototherapy methods range from Polaroid transfer and emulsion photocopy transfer; cyanotype printing; scripting and role play through video production; Luminous emulsions on paper, wood, metal, and ceramic; simple collage from magazine cutouts; and use of a photocopying machine to alter and distort images. Even Helen Landgarten (1993), an art therapist working in California, construed the efficacy of using photographic collage as an assessment tool when working with clients and created an assessment battery based on this medium.

The real advantage for students, however, can emanate from exploring one's own issues via creating a visual (albeit photographic/pictorial) genogram. This photographic snapshot of one's family tree can often tell more than a symbolic lined drawing as outlined by McGoldrick and Gerson (1985). As well, a timeline, which outlines nodal events (such as birth, death,

Figure 9-1. Stevens' quilt.

marriage, divorce, traumas, etc.) generally accompanies the genogram and serves to clarify life events. In fact, two of my past students continued to explore this concept in their final theses (Garlock, 1996; Stevens, 2001). Stevens' visual exploration literally was captured in a large quilted family tree and pillow shams of cyanotype images, which included images of birth announcements, personal letters, newspaper articles, as well as familial portraits. As well, she retuned home in order to include her family members in some of the sewing of the quilt and literally collaborated with them in the interlacing of their familial tapestry.

A visual representation can also affect one's view of import. For example, which photographs or even magazine cutouts does one use to represent his or her family members? And if variations are suggested, such as a directive like "cut out photographs of animals that represent each of your family members and construct a genogram," that, too, can offer up newfound information on one's perspective. Whether I am working with students or my own clients, I always start from a family systems platform. That seems to set the format of viewing oneself *not* as an identified patient (IP as referred to in the psychobabble literature) but more aptly as a *cog* within a system. When clients internalize themselves in this way, there is less blame involved: instead, they can merely see themselves as a symptom, which has brought the family system into the path towards recovery. Viewing oneself and others in degrees of wellness as opposed to dis-ease (as I like to call it) is less toxic, co-creative and a healthier response then dwelling in the darker spaces of blame, guilt, and shame.

In one such exercise, my students took a series of Polaroid images and were asked to eliminate the one that they most liked and least liked. Then, after selecting those pictures, they were asked to do some work around those images. The following image, used with the permission of my student, Jessica, is a stunning example of exactly how we continue to "carry around" those parts of ourselves that we dislike. In the Polaroid photograph below, Jessica first removed the emulsion backing (with warm water) and then rubbed off areas that she wished to be viewed as transparent. Next, she folded this image up and placed a string through it and contained it with a snap. And thus it appeared to be a tiny, sealed pocketbook. This obvious transformation into a small (yet, tightly sealed container for emotions) was the pinnacle of a transitional object.

Jessica's creation of a pocketbook was the epitome of such a concept; moreover, this container as a source of value (purse) was astoundingly perceptible even to her; she continued to value that which she liked least about herself, instead of throwing it away or discarding it in some other manner. That allowed for productive introspection for Jessica as well as her classmates.

In another assignment, I asked my students to create a personal box from any image and medium. One student, Joy, created a box that was a functional pincushion disguised as a bed. The cyanotype image chosen of her mother, flanked on both sides by Joy and her sibling, was an interesting selection. Since the very first day of class, the images, which Joy presented, exposed her pain from the internal fissure created by her parents' divorce. Joy revealed that her mother had been a seamstress. When she presented this piece, a personal box outfitted as a gift for her mother, the real contribution unraveled for Joy during that class: Joy was putting this issue to bed.

In another assignment, students were asked to take five Polaroid or digital images of themselves by directing a partner to photograph them. This opportunity to "direct" the shot as well as be the object is rather different from being behind the camera. While I have written about the healthy dissociative properties that an artist moves through when creating a work of art (Horovitz, 1999), adding a camera to the artistic arsenal certainly compounds the voyeuristic perspective. When asked to be on the other side, all kinds of issues arise, just from the directive itself. Her creation was a working, moving doll composed of various body parts, which she assembled with brass fasteners. The central component, a complete image of Megan, spoke to her sense of

Figure 9-2. Jessica's purse.

wellness—that is, being able to ingest a whole image (albeit holistic) of herself. This was quite affirming to Megan as she and others prattled on about its inner meaning.

In sampling the possibilities of Luminous transfer emulsion created from negatives or inverted images made in Photoshop software, I suggested possibilities beyond the use of paper. This allowed my students to explore this medium with copper and wood as well as fine watercolor paper. Making the emulsion permanent on such surfaces can be done with UVLS varnish, specifically designed for three-dimensional surfaces. My Luminous ceramic sample called "Sisters" is currently one way of working with past personal images.

## CLINICAL APPLICATIONS

In working with clients, oftentimes, I use photographic images, old movies or videos, and slides in order to retrieve memories long ago buried. This work sometimes leads to an art therapy session where the client might use these

Figure 9-3. Joy's bed.

images in order to create a pillow, a tee shirt, or sometimes even a quilt to honor people who have passed on. As well, those same photographic images can be digitized and stored on my computer in order to rework those graphics in such programs as Photoshop. Remaking images can be a restorative process. For example, when working with a client who is self-abusive, the process of enhancing, manipulating images and revealing information can be quite empowering in terms of how a client works through issues.

### INTERVENTION 1

Not everyone understands operating outside the parameters of four-walled therapeutic meetings. But working outside the confines of a therapeutic office can be quite supportive. An adolescent client, herein named "Brett," who suffered from self-injurious behavior (SIB), used both phototherapy techniques

Figure 9-4. Megan's doll.

as well as a digital camera to capture the world around him. Individual sessions consisted of taking walks in the woods and photographing nature as well as each other. The work seemed restorative and productive. When taking Brett out to a local donut shop one day, he began to develop this wonderful relationship with another patron. Every Tuesday that we came to the shop, this old woman would be seated opposite us reading her newspaper and eating her donut. Weeks passed by and we listened to her saga of her husband's recent hospitalization and coma state. Brett began photographing her. One day, he approached her with some of the photographs that he had taken

Figure 9-5. Sisters (by author).

of her and many other places. They talked for a full hour and both seemed more fully alive then when they had entered the shop. It was fascinating to see Brett in this altogether different environment. Here, he was polite, appropriate, and downright charming. But when returned to the residential treatment center, where he resided, like an animal about to be caged, he transmuted, becoming angry and resistant. To me, it was no surprise.

While countless examples of digital work ensued, one of the most unusual alterations was of Brett's eye. While I had photographed his eye (upon his direction), it wasn't until later that he confessed that its import had to do with me reflected in his eye. Clearly this was Brett's way of informing me that my "vision" of him was what mattered, no matter how others viewed his behavior.

Through further manipulation of the software, Brett changed the eye so that it appeared blackened, much like an eye would after being battered (see Figure 9-6). Because he had been terribly beaten by his biological father (aged 3), these kinds of images seemed to be somewhat cathartic for Brett. His need, for example, to carry around these photos became "transitional objects" between our meetings. Further work with this young man can be found in Horovitz, (1999).

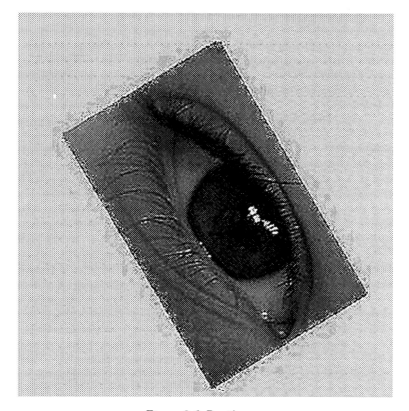

Figure 9-6. Brett's eye.

**INTERVENTION 2**

Still other applications can be used that are simpler should a practitioner not have access to digital equipment and/or computer software programs. A simple photocopy machine can be used to distort images by moving them over the glass when the light photographs the images to be copied. These copies can be reworked with multiple media. As well, even plain photocopies can be used pasted down on paper and a clinician need only suggest a simple directive such as: "If those images could say something, what would that be?" and suddenly a dialogue between images magically begins. In one such instance, when working with an aphasic client troubled by her marriage, that simple directive reduced her to tears and the newfound strength to rework these feelings through with her husband. The following "dialogue bubbles" were the impetus to that work (see Figure 9-7).

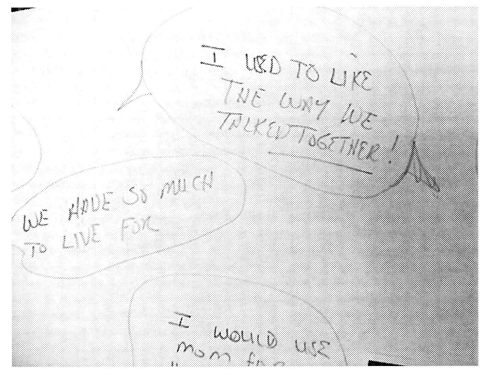

Figure 9-7. Aphasic client's work.

**INTERVENTION 3**

Still another client, diagnosed with Asperger's syndrome and mental retardation has used countless methods of phototherapy to create images of her family system. Many have resulted in gifts as well as transitional objects for herself. In one breakthrough session, when merely looking at slides from "C's" past, she began to cry for the first time. She sobbed relentlessly for ten minutes and explained in between her tears, "I promise I will be good, if only they'll take me back." This heartbreaking confession led to much earnest work towards forgiveness and repentance with her family of origin. As well, there were more positive sessions, where "C" would offer up her art projects as gifts to her family members. Her ability to create these works of art reflected increased self-worth and individuation.

Figure 9-8 is an example of a tee shirt transfer, which she gave to her mother as an example of her desire to bond like she had in the past.

Figure 9-8. C's tee shirt transfer.

Indeed several transitional objects were created in order for "C" to comfort herself with her mother's image when she was not with her. Figure 9-9 is the same image transferred as a fabric image onto a pillow below.

These creations, while perhaps crude in their artistry, were completely crafted by the client. Such activities were not only affirming but also emotively comforting to the client in ways that more plastic mediums have not been. Tangible items embedded with emotions from the past have restorative properties that can be coddled, held, and slept with. It is difficult to sleep with a painting or a sculpture, but images such as these are transferable to the psyche in an altogether different fashion.

## CONCLUSION

As outlined above, photographic images of all types can be incorporated in both academic and clinical applications. The emotive quality charged through images can captivate and motivate the human psyche in ways that other media simply cannot. Perhaps it is because the evocative power of a

Figure 9-9. C's pillow.

photographic image can stir the soul back into a time long forgotten. Coupled with the power of technological advances such as those aforementioned, people can rework past images and their selves in the process. Phototherapy continues to progress just as surely as the human race does in its quest for continued development. As technology advances, so too does the palate of phototherapy.

# Chapter 10

# A SEARCH FOR MEANING: INNER AND OUTER EXISTENCE

> . . . we are veined possibilities.
>
> –Horovitz, 1999

It has been some time since I wrote the first edition of this book, ten years to be exact (Horovitz-Darby, 1994). And truthfully, I have grown in many ways. But my thirst for a deeper, spiritual connection has remained the same– unquenched. As I continue to yearn for new knowledge, question my existence, and that of my patients, I have reflected on what I wrote a decade ago and still stand by what I have written.

While my views on spirituality have altered and changed as I have grown, *even today,* while seeing a family dealing with the death of their daughter, I was struck again by how much humans war with God and/or the belief system in which they were raised. It matters not how one is reared–this spirit that humans wrestle with cuts across all societal strata. Spirituality, that force that animates human beings, knows no boundaries and doesn't distinguish between social classes. And so when bad things happen to good people, doubt sets in, questions are raised, and people struggle for meaning and sense.

## THE EFFECTS OF 9-11

While our world has changed dramatically due to technological upgrades, Internet access, and instant global communication, humankind continues to be transformed by myriad events. Nonetheless, on September 11, 2001, something changed in America. On that notorious day, Americans were held hostage to a heinous, terrorist attack and as a nation, the people are still spinning from the insult. Confidence, security, and freedom were stripped away. Instead, humanity was left forever tainted. As a culture, the American people were reduced to a hypervigilant posture, just short of full-blown paranoia. Yet, despite the atrocity of the terrorist attack that befell the United States, one aspect remained intact: faith to overcome this horror. The American people as a whole, as a faith community, refused to knuckle under. Instead, banners, flags, and spirit reigned supreme via patriotism and a "united we stand" mentality. People seemed to slow down, actually take notice of one another and for a moment, however brief, truly care.

But in the days that followed, my patients' anxieties, exacerbated by this condition, seemed to heighten. In between emptying overflowing wastebaskets filled with used tissues, like others, I was emotionally paralyzed by the events. Glued to the television (which I rarely watch), I reviewed the tragic events repeatedly. I vacillated between numbness and tears as I donned my clinical hat, parental hat, and finally my inner hat. Since my dearest family members reside in New York City, along with some very dear friends, I was emotionally controlled by these events. I felt hostage to my feelings, which ping-pong'ed like a rubber ball, bouncing between Anthrax scares and my siblings' pronounced anxiety. Like others touched by this tragedy, I was grateful that my family was alive but devastated by how truly this had changed their lives and the lives of my children. I emailed friends in the city, who like my brother (a medical doctor), were working in the trenches. And like me, they were overwhelmed by the shock and trauma that surrounded them. The caretakers of society were burning out. There was no one to take care of them as they were in such high demand. And in my own practice, there was no one to take care of me. These events elevated all of my mourning and loss issues and cemented the same in my patients. Neutrality as a clinical armament was outmoded by empathic relatedness. We were truly all in the same boat. But as I turned to history, I was reminded by the work of Victor Frankl (1984) who so valiantly pointed out that those who stood by idly during the holocaust died and those who optimistically took action survived.

And action has always been my stance as I have never been one to sit languidly by and watch. So when November neared and it was time for me to go to the annual American Art Therapy Association conference, I continued my plans to go. Naturally, my children begged me not to travel and even my siblings questioned my decision. As a board member of the association, I was required to go, but in my heart, I *needed* to go. My inner hat sought that refuel and more importantly, I wanted to see my art therapist friends, for they are and always will be my faith community. While I thought the numbers would be down for the conference, surprisingly enough, they weren't. Instead, 833 seekers showed up, perhaps for the very same reason that I did: we needed each other in the wake of this horror that had surrounded our every day existence.

At this 32nd American Art Therapy Association conference (2001), the distinguished Thomas Moore was the keynote speaker. This guru of spirituality likened the need for art therapists to SWAT teams. His keynote address was funny, acerbic, and completely centered. His genuine humanity was a gift and his keen sense of humor was exactly what we needed. Like Norman Cousins' panacea for cancer (medicinal laughter), Thomas Moore's model was attempting the same: he recognized the healer's need to be healed.

What causes a community, a country for that matter, to band together and develop a renewed sense of faith? What triggers a people to look inward and take stock in what is truly important in life? What activates a civilization to return to a more ordered and spiritual existence? And why does it take a monstrous act to propel people into a civilized and cohesive lot? Why must a tragedy instill this kind of responsiveness in the human condition? Why can it not flourish without such a pivotal state of events? I suppose there really is no one answer to these quandaries, but it does make me realize that now more than ever, people are truly searching for meaning in their lives.

After this state of events, numerous books popped up on the tragedy as well as myriad web sites including this one: http://www.politicsandprotest .org. And while many of the above sites may have eased the concern of the masses, returning to my work was and always will be a source of solace for me (Horovitz, 1999). So I continued to make art. While this may not save the world or lead to a cure for biochemical warfare, art clearly is a major contribution, especially in the wake of the aforementioned events.

After that infamous day, I was struck by the numerous drawings of children shown on the television and plastered on magazine covers. Words were not necessary: the pictures told the whole story. Children, no matter what society they hailed from (be it from the war ridden Afghanistan or the family members of the World Trade Center and Pentagon), bore identical messages *and* in the exact same language. Communication, religion—these were not barriers. No here, amongst the crayon boxes and paint trays, language was one and the same . . . it was the language of art. Art was the universal spokesperson for the pain of our grieving nations and world. Mourning and loss were lit by the colors of the human palette. The color of our skin, the religious beliefs that we held, these all paled in comparison to the magical and healing power of art.

Artistic responses showed up everywhere: in memorials strewn with flowers and candles, in drawings and paintings, in quilts of remembrance, in pictures taken, in web sites created, in musical benefits. Artistic measures were underlining the very fabric of society that had been ripped out. A new weft of humanity became the tapestry of our existence.

While I wrote about the "call to art" in my second book (Horovitz, 1999), the concept of this extending into the fabric of society was always a hope. Perhaps it takes a great tragedy to move a people toward such an end. Unfortunate as that may be, any nodal event (be it positive or negative) that moves humans towards a more civilized existence is a welcome refuge. The sanctuary of art continues to be a safe haven, asylum of "soulution" (Horovitz, 1999), and necessary well spring from which I continue to operate. Perhaps it is here that, in fact, I am grounded in spirituality. If spirituality is in fact tethered to Creation, then art must be the religion to which I am bound.

Art does inform the fabric of my existence. It matters not what course it takes–written, spoken, painted, drawn, sculpted or even now, edited as a movie on my computer. However I am able to witness the miracle of art underscoring my animation really doesn't matter. Just as long as art pulses into the very fabric of my being, that is what truly gauges my existence. And if as a clinician, a writer, an artist, a mother, a teacher, a sister, a daughter, or a friend, I can instill this in others, well then, I know I am doing my job.

## MISTAKES THAT GROUND ME

Art is always a surprise to me. I remember when Edith Kramer was my mentor, she used to recall to me the importance behind the "happy accidents," which occurred in the enchantment of the art. Mistakes *never* transpired, no these were unconscious communications, otherwise disguised as the preconscious undertakers of our selves.

And while I am a proponent of this ideology when this so called "flaw" occurs in the work of my clients, sometimes, taking a dose of my own medicine is not always as palatable as one would hope.

Recently, when working on my own mourning and loss issues surrounding my father's untimely death, I happened upon a torn and tattered Raggedy Ann doll that I passed daily. On the stairwell to my basement, housed in a plastic baggie, was the remaining portions of the only doll, which my father had bought for me, albeit at the ripe old age of 18.

More attracted to erector sets and all things mechanical as a child, I never had dolls. But long ago, when my father was visiting me at college in Vermont, we happened upon this handmade, Raggedy Ann doll with an "I love you" embroidered over her heart. When I asked my father if he would buy it for me, he was all too pleased to do so and knew full well why I had asked him to be the buyer of the object. I loved that doll and all the metaphor that it invoked.

And it always rested comfortably on the pillow shams of my bed from that day forward. So when my infant daughter took a shining to it, long after my father's untimely death, naturally I gave it to her. This Raggedy Ann doll, which substituted as a token of my father's long gone affection, suddenly became a transitional object for my daughter. It accompanied her everywhere and she couldn't sleep or go on vacation without it. So when that doll was loved to the point of losing its limbs, we took it to a nearby doll maker who fashioned new parts for it. And when the body fell open again, we took it back for an upgrade. But when it broke apart at the seams a third time and the chest was ripped open and the "I love you" spilt asunder, I asked my daughter, then aged 10, who still couldn't sleep without this doll, if she would let the legs be used to fashion a new doll for her. And I asked her if she wouldn't mind if I kept the remains for myself. Knowing how much that doll meant to me, Kaitlyn was now old enough to understand its symbolic meaning for me. So she agreed, happily taking the legs to our doll maker friend, who created her a new doll, using the original roots, the legs of my doll, for her new Raggedy Ann.

Naturally, this whole scenario reminded me of my favorite book of all time. As a child, my mother never read to me. While she was an avid reader, we were left to our own devises, especially when she was often hospitalized for her manic depressive bouts. So during grade school, I made daily visits to the library. Too shy to ask where the children's section was, I seated myself at the nearest sitting room and combed through the shelves of the books above this arrangement. At age eight, I had read the entire Shakespeare collection and by nine, I finally wandered into the poetry section. It wasn't until age 10, that I actually located the children's section and happily read *Little Women* for the first time. But I never really found the childhood stories that most children were reared on. No, somehow, *Charlotte's Web, The Magician's Nephew,* and such classics as these never made it into my hands. But when my children were born, suddenly, I had an excuse to delve into fairytales and classic stories. Among the ones that I read was *The Velveteen Rabbit* by Margery Williams. This tiny 44-page wonder was probably one of the most profound books that I had ever encountered. Here was a story about becoming real and about being loved. In a famous line where the protagonists, Rabbit and Skin Horse, are discussing what makes an object real to a child, Skin Horse informs Rabbit exactly how this mystery occurs. He informs Rabbit:

> "Real isn't how you are made," said the Skin Horse.
> "It's a thing that happens to you. When a child loves you for a long, long time, not just to play with, but REALLY loves, then you become Real. It doesn't happen all at once. You become. It takes a long time. Generally, by the time you are Real, most of your hair has been loved off, and your eyes drop out and get loose in the joints and very shabby. But these things don't matter at all, because once you are Real you can't be ugly, except to people who don't understand." (1975, p. 17)

So when my child invested her energy into that beloved Raggedy Ann, it in fact had become a stand in for my love and this revered doll had in turn

Figure 10-1. Family (by author).

been the same for me. It had comforted me in times when my father could not be there and when my mother was unavailable, which for me had been often.

So when this doll eventually shredded and its heart wall had been split open by time, something in me had to salvage this object before there was nothing left. But years had gone by before I could face what was swelling up inside of me. I must have passed this doll, encased in its protective, plastic sleeve for years before I decided one day to finally pick it up. On that fateful day, I took it out of its plastic guard, masking taped it to a canvas, and began to paint an image of what was left of that time, of those feelings, long buried, and of that hurt that still rattled so deeply inside me. I needed to finally paint out my pain; I needed to make sense of it all—my father's death, my mother's brain damage that ensued in the related accident, the hole that was inside me so black and dark, and deep.

And so I painted. And while painting that work, I also combed through pictures of my family. Much later, one made it to a ceramic tile (Figure 10-1) and now adorns my office wall, to remind me of a time when we pretended to be whole.

Figure 10-2. Dad's shadow.

While working on the canvas of the Raggedy Ann doll, I came across an old slide that my father had taken of me; his figure was plainly visible in the shadow (Figure 10-2). For weeks, I painted this image onto the canvas alongside the Raggedy Ann as well as other images of my childhood, but the shadow of my father continued to haunt me as I added it to the canvas alongside other childhood images.

So one night, around two in the morning, I took some black paint and covered over those photographic shadows lurking in my heart, deadening my

Figure 10-3. All that's left you (by author).

canvas. And as I stood back and saw the paradox of what I had created, I realized that by painting out these mistakes and adding this "happy accident" of black paint, I had finally achieved what I was after. The strength of the black paint against the fragility of that Raggedy Ann doll appeared like a keyhole to my psyche (Figure 10-3).

Later when I decided on the title (fashioned after the famous Simon and Garfunkel 1972 musical score, Bookends), "All That's Left You" further underscored the indelible hole imprinted on my reasoning. Finally I had put my own mourning and loss issue to bed. This issue, which I thought I had made peace with, would not rest until I resolved it through my art. And like my patients, sometimes it takes years to be ready for that work. It had been many years for me before I was ready to face that work—sixteen to be exact. While time does help in healing, sometimes, we are only ready to face our demons when we are ready. This work cannot be pushed, not in ourselves or in others.

So this painting serves as a reminder to always be in touch with that spot in my life that connects me to my senses. It is this work that ties me to my patients as we cross that unknown road together. The journey to our consciousness is paved with spiritual reminders of what we came from and how this history continues to form our biology in everything that we do. This culture, this fabric of our existence, is woven into every strand of our body and every nuance of our mind. It is our belief system after all, and in walking that roadway, lined with the cement of art, we discover ourselves anew, awakened, and spiritually ready for the exclamation, the cry that is and continues to be the call to art.

(*Author's note:* A CD-ROM can be ordered from the author's website at http://www.naz.edu/dept/art_therapy/index.html. This movie can be opened in QuickTime software loaded on most computers. I hope that this will provide a glimpse into the BATA and CATA assessment and for those practitioners, who choose to utilize it in their practice—a window of how one conducts this battery with others. It is my aspiration that this will be helpful in your practice and ministry of others. In the words of Edith Kramer, my greatest mentor, I hope you steady your course with your own work and remember the practice of "ever art.")

# APPENDIX

# Table 1

# TABLE OF COMPARATIVE NORMS

| Eras/Ages | Erikson | Piaget | Kohlberg | Lowenfeld/Brittain* | Horovitz | Fowler |
|---|---|---|---|---|---|---|
| Infancy (0–1.5 yrs) | Basic Trust *vs.* Basic mistrust (hope) | Sensorimotor Stage | | Scribble Stage: Beginning of Self-Expression (age 0–2 years) | | Stage 1 Intuitive/Projective; age 3–7 years |
| Early Childhood (2–6 yrs) | Autonomy *vs.* Shame and Doubt Initiative *vs.* Guilt (Purpose) | Preoperational or Intuitive | *Preconventional Level* 1. Heteronomous Morality | Preschematic Stage: First Representations (4–7 yrs) | | |
| Childhood (7–12 yrs) | Industry *vs.* Inferiority | Concrete Operational | 2. Instrumental exchange *Conventional level* 3. Mutual Interpersonal relationships | The Schematic Stage: Formed Concepts (age 7–9 yrs) | | Stage 2 Mythical Literal Stage; Age 8–12 (but can dominate through adolescence) |
| Adolescence (13–21 yrs) | Identity *vs.* Role Confusion (fidelity) | Formal Operational | 4. Social System and Conscience | The Gang Age: Dawning Realism (age 9–12 yrs) | | Stage 3, Synthetic-Conventional Faith; adolescence through adulthood |

| Young Adulthood (21–35 yrs) | Intimacy vs. Isolation (Love) | *Postconventional Principled Level* 5. Social contract, individual rights | Pseudo-Naturalistic Stage: Age of Reasoning (age 12–14 yrs.) | Stage 4 Individuative-Reflective; Late adolescence-adulthood |
|---|---|---|---|---|
| Adulthood (35–60 yrs) | Generativity vs. Stagnation (Care) | | Adolescent Art: Period of Decision (14–17 yrs) | Stage 5 Conjunctive Faith; @ midlife |
| Maturity (60+) | Integrity vs. Despair (Wisdom) | Universal Ethical Principles | | Stage 6 Universaling Faith; wisdom, transformation, Selfless acts are hallmarks of this stage (age Undetermined) |
| | | | | Adult Stage: Formation in the World (age 18–adulthood) |
| | | | | Artistic Stage: Formed Art Any age (generally in adolescent through adulthood) |

i Re: the Stages of Development as outlined by Lowenfeld and Brittain: please see below:

i While Lowenfeld and Brittain do not describe this as a stage, **Brain Injured Stage** can occur at any age, and I have described this stage in my lectures as consisting of organic qualities, where objects float on the page (e.g. lack of order and ungrounded quality to the artwork is pervasive in the representations, be they two or three-dimensional in design.)

As well, since they do not hallmark the **Adult or Artistic Stages of Development**, I do, since I feel that these stages vary dramatically from the Adolescent period, the last stage, which they described.

# Table 2

# BELIEF ART THERAPY ASSESSMENT

## History Taking

Name, Age, Religion, and Career (if applicable).

*Questions:*

1. What is you religious affiliation?
2. Have there ever been any changes in your religious affiliation?
3. When did these changes take place (if applicable) and what were the circumstances that caused this change?
4. What is the level of your present involvement with your church, temple, or faith community?
5. What is your relationship with your pastor, rabbi, priest, or spiritual leader?
6. Do you have any religious practices that you find particularly meaningful?
7. What kind of relationship do you have with God if applicable?
8. What gives you special strength and meaning?
9. Is God involved in your problems? (Depending on how this is answered, you might want to clarify whether or not the subject involves God in his problems and/or blames God for his problems)
10. Have you ever had a feeling of forgiveness from God?

***N.B. All of these questions need not be asked and also depending on personality and psychological parameters, one may choose to skip this section altogether since it may exacerbate psychosis.***

## First Directive

Please remember that the manner in which a subject is presented with the request to delineate his belief system is all important. The administrant could begin the topic by stating something like, "Have you ever thought about how the universe was created and who or what was responsible for its creation?" Then once a dialogue regarding the topic is started, the interviewer could actually lead into the art task itself by stating, "Many people have a belief in God; if you also have a belief in God, would you draw, paint, or sculpt what God **means** to you." The instruction should be stated exactly as it is written since any deviation from the original intent might imply subject bias. The reason for the words **"means to you"** is essential. Direct representation may be offensive in some religious/cultural background.

If a prospective subject is an atheist or agnostic, the administrant might simply request that the subject attempt to delineate what it is he or she believes in. If the subject believes in nothing, one could ask the subject to define that in the media.

However, if the subject defines himself/herself as an agnostic/atheist, some questions might be:

1. Have you ever believed in God?

If the answer is yes, one might then ask:

2. What caused you to no longer believe in God and when did that occur?

(One could still ask questions 5, 8, and 10 as stated above)

## Post Assessment Interrogation

1. Could you explain what you have made and what that means to you?
2. Have you ever witnessed or seen God as you have delineated your artwork?
3. How do you feel about what you have just made?

Moreover, let the subject talk freely about his or her artwork and record significant verbal associates to the work produced.

## Second Directive

Some people create the opposite of God simultaneously with the above directive of creating what God means to them. If, however, the subject does not, then state, "Some people believe that there is an opposite of God. If you believe there is an opposite force, could you also draw, paint or sculpt that?"

Naturally the same post assessment interrogation can proceed following the latter request.

The BATA can be scored cognitively according to Lowenfeld and Brittain (1975) using the same parameters that are outlined in the CATA assessment (Horovitz, 1988, 1999).

# BIBLIOGRAPHY

Ahlskog, G. (1990). Atheism and pseudo-atheism in the pychoanalytic paradigm. *Psychoanalysis and Contemporary Thought. 13* (1), 53–77.

Allen R. J., & Yarian R.A. (1981. The domain of health. *Health Education, 12* (4), 3–5.

Alschuler, R., & Hattwick, B. (1947). *Painting and personality.* Chicago: University of Chicago Press.

Anechiarico, B. (1990). Understanding and treating sex offenders from a self-psychological perspective : The missing piece. *Clinical Social Work Journal, 18* (4), 281–292.

Arrington, D. (1991). Thinking systems–seeing systems: An integrative model for systemically oriented art therapy. *The Arts in Psychotherapy,* an international journal, Vol 18 (3): 201–211.

Asch, S. (1985). Depression and demonic possession: The analyst as exorcist. *Hillside Journal of Clinical Psychiatry. 7* (2), 149–164.

Ashbrook, J.B. (1971). *Be/come Community.* Valley Forge, PA: Judson Press.

Assagioli, R. (1965). *Psychosynthesis: A manual of principles and techniques.* New York: Viking Penguin.

Assagioli, R. (1989). Self-realization and psychological disturbances. In S. Grof, & C. Grof (Eds.), *Spiritual emergency: When personal transformation becomes a crisis.* Los Angeles: Jeremy P. Tarcher, pp. 27–48.

Beck, C.J. (1989). *Every day Zen: Love and work.* New York: Harper and Row.

Bell, J.E. (1961). *Family group therapy: A method for the psychological treatment of children, adolescents, and their parents.* Washington, D.C.: U.S. Department of Health, Education, and Welfare, Public Health Monograph No. 64, U.S. Government Printing Office.

Bell, J.E. (1974). *Family therapy.* New York: Aronson.

Bergin, A.E. (1991). Values and religious issues in psychotherapy and mental health. *American Psychologist.* 46, 394–403.

Bowlby, J. (1951). *Maternal care and mental health.* Geneva: WHO Technical Monograph Series, No. 2.

Bruch, H. (1973). *Eating disorders.* New York: Basic Books.

Buck, J.N. (1950). *Administration of the H-T-P test.* Proceedings of the Workshop held at Veterans Administration Hospital, Richmond, VA: March 31, April 1, 2.

Buck, J.N. (1966). *The House-Tree-Person Technique: Revised manual.* Beverly Hills, CA: Western Psychological Services.

Burns, R.C., & Kaufmann, S.H. (1972). *Actions, styles and symbols in Kinetic Family Drawings (K-F-D)*. New York: Brunner/Mazel.

Capell, E. (1991). *The emergence of idiosyncratic religious and demonic themes in art therapy; Implications for treatment*. Unpublished thesis submitted in partial fulfillment of the requirements for the Certificate of Completion Rochester, NY: Hillside Children's Center's Clinical Training Program in Creative Arts Therapy,

Capell, E. (1991). *Recurrent themes in the artwork of a sexually deviant adolescent with autistic psychopathy, and implications for treatment*. Unpublished paper, Rochester, NY: Hillside Children's Center.

Cericola, C.C. (1975). *Religious imagery as manifested in art work of schizophrenics of the Catholic religion*. Philadelphia: Hahnemann Medical College (Creative Arts Therapy Program).

Chandler, C.K., Holden, J.M., & Kolander, C.A. (1992). Counseling for spiritual wellness: Theory and practice. *Journal of Counseling and Development*. Nov/Dec Vol. 71, 168–175.

Chittister, J.D. (1993). Work: A pathway to something deeper. *Liguorian*, September, 4–9.

Cohen, S., & Wills, T.A. (1985). Stress, social support, and the buffering hypothesis. *Psychological Bulletin*. 98: 310–57.

Coles, R. (1990). *The spiritual life of children*. Boston: Houghton Mifflin.

Dearing, T. (1983). *God and healing of the mind: A spiritual guide to mental health*. South Plainfield, NJ: Bridge Publications.

Dombeck, M., & Karl, J. (1987). Spiritual issues in mental health. *Journal of Religion and Health*. Fall, Vol. 26 (3) 183–197.

Eadie, B.J. (1992). *Embraced by the light*. California: Gold Leaf Press.

Edwards, E. (1968). Family day care in a community action program. *Children*. 15, 55–58.

Ekstein, R. (1959). Thoughts concerning the nature of the interpretive process. In Levitt M. (Ed): *Readings in psychoanalytic psychology*. New York: Appleton-Century-Crofts, 266–281.

Ellison, C.W. (1983). Spiritual well-being: Conceptualization and measurement. *Journal of Psychology and Theology*. Win., Vol. 11 (4) 330–334.

Ellison, C. G. (1991). Religious involvement and subjective well-being. *Journal of Health and Social Behavior*. Mar., Vol. 32 (1), 80–99.

Erikson, E. (1963). *Childhood and society* (2d ed.). New York: Norton.

Fowler, J.W. (1981). *Stages of faith: The psychology of human development and the quest for meaning*. San Francisco: Harper.

Fowler, J.W., & Keen, S. (1978). *Life-Maps: Conversations on the journey of faith*. Waco, TX: Word Books.

Frank, J.D., & Frank, J.B. (1991). *Persuasion and healing: A comparative study of psychotherapy* (3d ed.). Baltimore: John Hopkins University Press.

Frankl, V. (1984). *Man's search for meaning: An introduction to logotherapy*. New York: Simon and Schuster.

Fryear, J.L., & Corbit, I. E. (1992). *Photo Art Therapy: A Jungian perspective*. Springfield, IL: Charles C Thomas.

Garlock, L.R. (1996). *A visual journey.* Rochester, NY: Nazareth College, unpublished thesis.

Gartner, J., Larson, D.B., & Allen, G.D. (1991). Religious commitment and mental health: A review of empirical literature. *Journal of Psychology and Theology.* Special Issue: Perspectives in theory and research, Spr., Vol. 19 (1), 6–25.

Gilby, R., Wolf, L., & Goldberg, B. (1989). Mentally retarded adolescent sex offenders: A survey and pilot study. *Canadian Journal of Psychiatry,* 34, 542–548.

Gordon, J.S. (1990). Holistic medicine and mental health practice. *American Journal of Orthopsychiatry,* Jul., Vol. 60 (3), 357–36.

Guerin P., & Pendagast, E. (1976). Evaluation of family system and genogram. In P. J. Guerin (Ed.), *Family Therapy: Theory and Practice.* New York: Gardner Press, 450–464.

Halpern, W.I., & Kissel, S. (1976). *Human resources for troubled children.* New York: John Wiley & Sons.

Hammer, E.F. (1990). (1990). *Reaching the affect: Style in the psychodynamic therapies.* Northvale, NJ: Jason Aronson.

Harding, M. E. (1971). *Woman's mysteries.* New York: G.P. Punam's Sons.

Harvey, M.A. (1984). Family therapy with deaf persons: The utilization of an interpreter. *Family Process,* 23, (June) 205–221.

Henricson-Cullberg, M. (1984). God as holding function—a religious conversion. 9th Nordic Psychoanalytic Congress: Interpretation—Holding: Alternative or Complement? (Saltsjobaden, Sweden ) *Scandinavian Psychoanalytic Review,* 7 (2), 184–194.

Hertz, J.H. (Ed.). (5751 or 1990). *Pentateuch and haftorahs.* Hebrew text/English translation and comments, London: Soncino Press.

Hettler, W. (1979). *Six dimensions of wellness.* Stevens Point, WI: National Wellness Institute, University of Wisconsin—Stevens Point.

Hettler, W. ( 1991). Hettler urges counselors to set example for society. *Guidepost,* 17–18.

*Holy Bible in King James version.* (1985). TN: Dugan Publishers.

Horovitz, E.G. (1999). *A leap of faith: The call to art.* Springfield, IL: Charles C Thomas.

Horovitz-Darby, E.G. (1988). Art therapy assessment of a minimally language skilled deaf child. Chapter 11 in *Mental health assessment of deaf clients: Special conditions,* Proceedings from the 1988 University of California's Center on Deafness Conference, ADARA, 115–127.

Horovitz-Darby, E.G. (1991). Family art therapy within a deaf system. *Arts in Psychotherapy,* Vol. 18, 251–261.

Horovitz-Darby, E.G. (1992). Countertransference: implications in treatment and post treatment. *Arts in Psychotherapy,* Vol. 19, 379–389.

Horovitz-Darby, E.G. (1994). *Spiritual art therapy: An alternate path.* Springfield, IL: Charles C Thomas.

James, H. (1917). *The middle years.* New York: Scribner.

Jaoudi, M. (1993). *Christian & Islamic spirituality: Sharing a journey.* New York: Paulist Press.

Jung, C.G. (1965). *Memories, dreams, and reflections*. New York: Vintage Books.

Jung, C.G. (1966). *Collected works*. Vol. 15. Princeton, NJ: Princeton University Press.

Junge, M.B., & Linesch, D. (1993). Our own voices: New paradigms for art therapy research. *Arts in Psychotherapy,* Vol. 20 (1), 61–67.

Kohlberg, L. (1969). Stage and sequence: The cognitive developmental approach to socialization. In D.A. Goslin (Ed.) *Handbook of socialization theory and research*. Chicago: Rand McNally.

Kohut, H. (1977). *The restoration of the self.* New York: International Universities Press.

Kramer, E. (1975). *Art as therapy with children*. New York: Schocken Books.

Krauss, D. (1979). Phototherapy course offered at Kent State (edited by B. Zakem). *Photo Therapy Quarterly.,* 2 (1), 12–13.

Krauss, D.A., & Fryear, J.L. (1983). *Phototherapy in mental health*. Springfield, IL: Charles C Thomas.

Landgarten, H.B., & Lubber, D. (Eds.) (1991). *Adult art psychotherapy: Issues and applications*. New York: Brunner/Mazel.

Landgarten, H.B. (1993). *Magazine photo collage: A multicultural assessment and treatment technique*. New York: Brunner/Mazel.

LaVietes, R., Cohhen, R., Reens, R., & Ronall, R. (1965). Day treatment center and school: Seven years experience. *American Journal of Orthopsychiatry*, 35, 368–482.

Levinson, D. J. (1978). *Seasons of a man*. New York: Alfred A Knopf.

Lowenfeld, V., & Brittain,W.L. (1975). *Creative and mental growth* (6th ed.). New York: MacMillan.

Maltsberger, J.T., & Buie, D.H. (1974). Countertransference hate in the treatment of suicidal patients. *Archives of General Psychiatry*, Vol. 30, May, 625–633.

Marano Geiser, R. (1990). Through the looking glass: II. Impact on the artist self. *Art Therapy,* Fall, 110–113.

Maslow, A. (1971). *Farther reaches of human nature*. New York: Viking.

Maton. K.I. (1989). The stress-buffering role of spiritual support: Cross sectional and prospective investigations. *Journal for the Scientific Study of Religion,* 28 (3): 310–323.

May, G.G. (1982). *Simply sane: The spirituality of mental health*. New York: Crossroad.

Meissner, S.J. (1992). The psychology of belief systems. *Psychoanalysis and Contemporary Thought,* 15, 99–128.

McGoldrick, M., & Gerson, R. (1985). *Genograms in family assessment*. New York: W.W. Norton.

McDargh, J. (1983). *Psychoanalytic object relations theory and the study of religion*. Latham, MD: University Press.

McNiff, S. (1981). *The arts and psychotherapy*. Springfield, IL: Charles C Thomas.

McNiff, S. (1992). *Art as medicine*. Boston & London: Shambhala.

Moon, B.L. (1990). *Existential art therapy: The canvas mirror*. Springfield, IL: Charles C Thomas.

Moon, C. (1992). *Images of God: The effects of abuse on God representations*. Las Vegas, NV: Presentation at the American Art Therapy Association Conference.

Moon, C. (1994). Mystery: The Guiding Image. *Art Therapy,* Vol. 11, (1), 18–22.

Moore, T. (1992). *Care of the soul: A guide for cultivating depth and sacredness in everyday life.* New York: Harper-Collins.

Minuchin, S., Rosman, B.L., & Baker, L. (1978). *Psychosomatic families: Anorexia nervosa in context.* Cambridge, MA: Harvard University Press.

Neumann, E. (1959). *Art and the creative unconscious.* Princeton, NJ: Princeton University Press.

Natal, J. (1994). A great photo opportunity (interviewed by Urbanic, K.). *Connection.* Winter/Spring, Vol. 7, No, 2, 2–4.

Newman, J., & Pargament, K.I. (1987). The role of religion in the problem solving process. Louisville, KY: Paper presented at the Society for the Scientific Study of Religion.

Peck, M. S. (1983). *People of the lie: The hope for healing human evil.* New York: Simon and Schuster.

Piaget, J. (1969). *The psychology of the child.* New York: Basic Books.

Prasinos, S. (1992). Spiritual aspects of psychotherapy. *Journal of Religion and Health,* Vol. 31, No. 1, Spring, 41–52.

Price, A.W. (1983). *The healing of nervous disorders by spiritual therapy.* Philadelphia: St. Steven's Church.

Ramseyer, J. (1990). Through the looking glass. III: Exploring the dark side through post-session artwork. *Art Therapy,* Fall, 114–117.

Rabin, A.I. (1965). *Growing up in the kibbutz.* New York: Springer.

Rubin, J.A. (1984). *The Art of Art Therapy.* New York: Brunner/Mazel.

Silver, R.A. (1992). *Silver Drawing Test of Cognitive and Creative Skills* (3d ed.). Sarasota, FL: Ablin Press.

Silver, R.A. (1992). *Draw A Story Test: Screening for depression.* Sarasota, FL: Ablin Press.

Simon, R. (1989). The spiritual program: its importance for mental health. *Studies in Formative Spirituality,* May Vol 10 (2), 157–170.

Simon, P., & Garfunkel, A. (1972). Bookends. *Simon and Garfunkel's greatest hits.* New York: Columbia Records.

Spilka, B., & Schmidt, G. (1983). General attribution theory for the psychology of religion: The influence on event character on attribution of God. *Journal for the Scientific Study of Religion,* 22: 326–39.

Spitz, R.A. (1965). *The first year of life: A psychoanalytic study of normal and deviant development of object relations.* New York: International Universities Press.

Steinfels, P. (1994). Psychiatrists' manual shifts stance on religious and spiritual problems. New York: *New York Times,* February 10, 1994.

Stevens, L.W. (2001). *Journal of a quilt, "family transition."* Rochester, NY: Nazareth College, unpublished thesis.

Sweet Burdette, R. (1990). *Writing towards wisdom: The writer as shaman.* Carmichael, Ca.: Helios House.

Tart, C.T. (1989). *Open mind, discriminating mind: Reflections on human possibilities.* San Francisco: Harper & Row.

Wadeson, H. (1990). Through the looking glass: I. When clients' tragic images illuminate the therapist's dark side. *Art Therapy,* Fall, 107–110.

Walls, C. (1991). Informal support from black churches and the well-being of elderly blacks. *Gerontologist,* Aug., Vol 31 (4), 490–495.

*We celebrate Missalette.* (1993). Schiller Park, IL: J.S.Paluch Company. Vol. 8, No. 3.

Weiser, J. (1993). *Phototherapy Techniques.* San Francisco: Jossey-Bass.

Williams, M. (1975). *The velveteen rabbit.* New York: Avon Books.

Worthington, E.L., Jr. Religious faith across the life span: Implications for counseling and research. *Counseling Psychologist,* 17, 555–612.

Worthington, E.L., Jr. (1986). Religious counseling: A review of published empirical research. *Journal of Counseling and Development,* 64, 421–31.

Wright, S., Pratt, C., & Scmall, V. (1985). Spiritual support for caregivers of dementia patients. *Journal of Religion and Health,* 24: 31–38.

Young, H.S. (1984). Practicing RET with Bible Blue Belt Christians. *British Journal of Cognitive Psychotherapy,* 2 (2), 60–76.

Young, H.S. (1984) Teaching rational self-concepts to tough customers. *British Journal of Cognitive Psychotherapy,* 2 (2), 77–98.

# NAME INDEX

Stevens, L.W., 155, 185
Sweet Burdette, R., 148, 149, 185

**T**

Tart, C.T., 18, 23, 185
Tolstoy, 144

**U**

Ueland, B., 147

**W**

Wadeson, H., 49, 64, 185
Walls, C., x, 186

Ward, L.B., 116
Weiser, J., 153, 186
Williams, M., 169, 186
Wills, T.A., 17, 186,
Wilson, L., 116,
Wolf, L., 105, 183
Worthington, E.L., 16, 26, 186
Wright, S., 17, 186

**Y**

Yarian, R.A., 17, 181
YMCA, 111
Young, H.S., 18, 186

# SUBJECT INDEX

## A

Abandonment, 112, 134
Abbot, 77
Abreaction, 7
Agnostic, 28, 41, 62, 66, 69, 71, 72, 76, 77, 93, 138
AIDS, 114, 121
Ambivalence, 116
American Art Therapy Association, 149, 166, 167
Angel, 75, 116
Angel, fallen, 54
Anorectic, xi, xix, xx, 111, 115
Anorexia, 134, 136
Anthrax, 166
Asperger's Syndrome, xi, 99, 153, 162
Aphasia, xi, 153, 161
Anxiety, xiii, xvi
Approach-avoidance, 14, 93, 120
Arab, 144
Archetypes, 21, 62, 63, 149, 153
Art, xiv, xvi, 19, 62, 68, 80, 84, 95, 168
Artistic Stage, 62, 70, 177
Art therapist, xi, 23, 32, 65, 94, 95, 99, 101, 105, 106, 149, 166
Art Therapy, x, xi, xiii, xiv, xvi, xix, 8, 9, 11, 26, 66, 86, 91, 94, 101, 105, 146, 157
Asceticism, 144
Asexual, 114, 133
Asperger's syndrome, 99
Assessment, 12, 16, 31, 32, 35, 93, 99, 102, 105, 106
Atheist, 28, 41, 66, 67, 69, 70, 93
Atonement, 95, 105
Autistic, 99, 153

## B

Baptism, 10, 24, 82, 84, 113, 127, 138
Baptist, 40
Belief, xx, 4, 7, 8, 9, 11, 12, 14, 16, 19, 23, 24, 26, 27, 31, 35, 37, 39, 41, 56, 57, 66, 68, 69, 71, 76, 77, 82, 84, 87, 88, 89, 94, 96, 98, 99, 102, 106, 122, 148, 149, 151, 165, 167, 173
Belief Art Therapy Assessment (BATA), viii, xi, xix, xx, 4, 8, 11, 12, 26, 27, 28, 29, 32, 41, 50, 64, 87, 88, 93, 94, 95, 96, 99, 100, 102, 105, 106, 116, 131, 173
Bible, 19, 20, 58
Biofeedback, 121, 127
Binge, 114, 115, 116, 119, 131, 136
Bipolar, 49
Blessed Mother Mary, 39
Borderline Personality, 107
Buddha, 77
Buddhist, 24, 66, 69, 76, 77, 78
Buddhist sutras, 20
Bulimic, xi, xix, xx, 111, 115

## C

CATA (Cognitive Art Therapy Assessment), xx, 94, 96, 97, 98, 116, 173
Cantor, 81
Castration anxiety, 136, 137
Catholicism, ix, 3, 142
Catholic, Roman, 41, 44, 72, 73, 95, 96, 112, 120, 123, 131, 145
Center for Ethics and Corporate Policy, 142
Christian, 24, 39, 53, 58, 79, 102, 130, 138, 141
Clonidine, 107

## Z

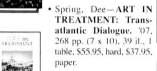

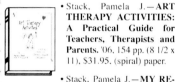

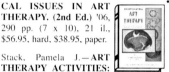

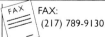